MUSIC FROM

CUBA

Mongo Santamaría,
Chocolate Armenteros
and Cuban Musicians in the
United States

CHARLEY GERARD

PRAEGER

Westport, Connecticut
London

Library of Congress Cataloging-in-Publication Data

Gerard, Charley.
    Music from Cuba : Mongo Santamaría, Chocolate Armenteros and Cuban musicians in
the United States / Charley Gerard.
        p. cm.
    Includes bibliographical references (p.) and index.
    ISBN 0–275–96682–8 (alk. paper)
    1. Musicians—Cuba. 2. Musicians—United States. 3. Cuban Americans—United
States—History and criticism. I. Title.

ML394.M86 2001
    780'.89'687291—dc21   00–045148

British Library Cataloguing in Publication Data is available.

Library of Congress Catalog Card Number: 00–045148
ISBN: 0–275–96682–8

First published in 2001

Praeger Publishers, 88 Post Road West, Westport, CT 06881
An imprint of Greenwood Publishing Group, Inc.
www.praeger.com

Printed in the United States of America

The paper used in this book complies with the
Permanent Paper Standard issued by the National
Information Standards Organization (Z39.48–1984).

10 9 8 7 6 5 4 3 2

Contents

Introduction

The dynamics of Cuban culture are central to the music that developed in the United States, and Cuban policies, both official and unofficial, have had a central role in the spread of Afro-Cuban music to the United States. The pioneers of stateside Cuban music like Mario Bauzá and Mongo Santamaría came to the United States because of Cuban racism. The Cuban Revolution sent many musicians out of the island, and the ensuing U.S. embargo kept the newest developments in Afro-Cuban music from all but a few connoisseurs. Subsequent policies like the *Mariel* boat lift brought more musicians to the States.

The paradox is that the Cuban roots of what is called Latin music and salsa have been obscured. Most of the popular Latin music performers in the United States such as Tito Puente, La India, Marc Anthony and Willie Colón are of Puerto Rican origin. Their music is no longer identified as Afro-Cuban. The term "salsa" was first attached to Latin music in the late 1960s by New Yorkers involved in the music's promotion—in particular, Gerry Masucci and his record label, Fania Records. They wanted to make it into something new. They believed it would have a better chance of gaining a huge audience if it were promoted like soul music: homegrown in the shadows of an urban landscape. From a marketing standpoint, it is easy to guess a few more reasons why they didn't want to call it "Afro-Cuban music." First, the term lacks advertising pizazz. Second, ascribing a nationality to the music might turn away non-Cubans. And finally, "Afro-Cuban music" was reminiscent of Machito and the Afro-Cubans, the music of the previous generation. The Cuban people as well as many Nuyorican artists disliked the new name because they believed that Fania was trying to pass off an old wine as if it were a new vintage. Some Cubans and Cuban Americans like Mongo Santamaría believed that the music businesspeople behind Latin music were taking credit away from Cuba. They resented them for succeeding in making a new generation of Latin music lovers unaware of the music's Cuban roots. Even the musicians were ignorant, according to percussionist Johnny Almendra:

The one thing that salseros forget is that every single rhythm that we play originated in Cuba. Unless you're playing bomba or plena. We play a tumbao and people forget *que eso es Cubano* ("that that is Cuban"). And the many variations of it as well. The people that taught us were the old Cubanos like Mongo, Peraza, Cándido, and Julian Cabrera. All those guys used to pull my ears: *"Mira, estás haciendo eso mal!"* ("Look, you're doing that badly!") . . . You have to acknowledge where this music came from. Yes, Puerto Rico has its own style of salsa, but its origins are from Cuba. We play it our way, with our Puerto Rican flavor, attitude, and influence, but the roots are still there in Cuba.[1]

Then there is the label "Latin jazz." One would think that Latin jazz, a shorthand for Latin American jazz, is a broad category that includes all the Spanish-speaking and perhaps even the Portuguese music of South America and the Caribbean. But Latin jazz is really more specific than that: it is really just Afro-Cuban influenced jazz. In Cuba, improvised music over an Afro-Cuban rhythm section is called descarga (literally, "discharge"). I guess it is fair to distinguish improvised music with solos in the jazz tradition as Latin jazz, and improvised music in the tradition of Cachao (Israel Cachao López), Juan Pablo Torres or Chocolate Armenteros as descarga.

I began this project with the idea of writing a biography of Mongo Santamaría and his generation of musicians. These are remarkable lives. Born in the poor rumbero districts of Havana where percussion groups and Santería bembes filled the streets with energy and aché nearly every day and night, Santamaría, Armando Peraza, Cándido, Francisco Aguabella and Julito Collazo have lived for over seven jam-packed decades. They have all gone far from the poverty-stricken days of their youths. Early in their careers all of these musicians found acclaim on the Cuban musical landscape but not much money—$10 for about seven hours of performing was the best they could hope for. They knew they would never find much remuneration, acclaim and respect in their native land so they left as soon as they got the chance.

These musicians did not fit easily into American communities. They were not welcomed by the white Cuban refugees who began arriving in the United States a decade after them. They could not share wholeheartedly in the rabid anti-Castroism of their light-skinned fellow countrymen, since they knew that Castro, despite his shortcomings, was working to improve the lives of poor Afro-Cubans. They didn't mesh well with Puerto Rican salseros and Latin music dignitaries who promoted their music as if it were their own invention and seemingly were reluctant to acknowledge its Cuban roots. In the jazz world they were championed by everyone from Charlie Parker to Herbie Mann, but few in the jazz world really knew Cuban music.

I was excited to interview them because they are among the few living witnesses to Havana nightlife before Fidel Castro irrevocably changed it. What was it like living in an Afro-Cuban neighborhood where music and religious fiestas were ubiquitous, where gangs competed to see who had the best drummers? What was it like being stranded in the United States after the Cuban Revolution, with little hope of ever seeing family and friends again?

Over time, I realized that I wished to write about the issues of Cuban identity and the difficulties and rewards of moving to a new country using representatives from several generations of Cuban immigrants, instead of just those from Santamaría's generation. Also, I wanted to interview musicians with different musical experiences, instead of only congueros. The musicians who ended up having their stories told in this book were chosen because they were receptive to the idea and because I was given their names by mutual acquaintances. Marty Sheller, David Carp and Sam Bardfeld provided me with the contact information I desperately needed. Sam Bardfeld also introduced me to Richard Davies, an excellent trombonist active in Latin music who was writing his dissertation on Afredo "Chocolate" Armenteros. Davies contributed a chapter on this well-known Cuban American trumpeter. In addition, George Rivera, a former musician with an extensive knowledge of Latin music, contributed an interview of Jesús Caunedo.

Finally, I wish to thank Marty and Marilyn Sheller, Mossa Bildner, Sam Bardfeld, John Amira, Robin D. Moore, Judith Weinstock, Kay Whitney and Mitchell Levenberg for their comments and suggestions.

1

Stateside Cuban Music

Each generation of immigrants is confronted by an Americanized version of its native culture. Nowhere is this phenomenon more apparent than when it comes to cuisine, the art form of everyday life. One of the disappointments that nearly all immigrants share is their inability to recreate the cuisine of their native land: inevitably, there is a missing ingredient. In Mexico, dishes are completed by a sprinkling of fresh cheese (*queso fresco*). When Mexicans cross the border they find out that sour cream has been substituted, since *queso fresco*, an unpasteurized dairy product, is nearly impossible to find. And then there are cases in which taste buds change when people make their home on American shores. In Italy, spaghetti sauce is a side attraction; the main dish is the spaghetti itself. Italians come to United States and discover to their surprise that spaghetti is merely a foil for the sauce. Cuban Americans in the United States sometimes use black pepper, but it is not an ingredient in classic Cuban recipes.[1]

Some of the same processes that may alter national cuisines beyond recognition take place in music as well. Since the 1950s, Cuban music has sounded different, and meant something different, in the United States than in Cuba. These differences have accrued like sedimental layers of rock. The result is that stateside Cuban music has solidified; it has its own characteristics and has developed its own heritage. It is not simply a matter of whether stateside is better or worse than homegrown Cuban. It has become something different, with its own aesthetic.

The individual who made stateside Cuban music was Mario Bauzá, who designed a band with his brother-in-law Machito (Frank Grillo) that combined American swing with Afro-Cuban rhythms. Bauzá wanted a band that could play with the high level of disciplined musicianship expected of American musicians but also with a true Cuban flair. The band was dubbed Machito and the Afro-Cubans. Diverse musical influences came from within this band. The saxophone and trumpet sections were filled with jazz players, and the piano slot was occupied by someone who could mix in jazz elements with traditional Cuban sounds. The rhythm section included Afro-Cuban percussionists and New Yorkers of Puerto Rican descent who wanted to learn the Afro-Cuban idiom.

One of them was Tito Puente. The background of the perennial band-leader is a perfect metaphor for what made him a central figure in stateside Cuban music. He grew up speaking English on the street and Spanish at home. As a young man, he learned big band drumming. As a teenager, he joined Machito's orchestra and learned how to play Cuban popular rhythms. Later, he made it his business to acquaint himself with Afro-Cuban culture. A trained musician who read music fluently, he took the study of the oral tradition of Afro-Cuban folkloric music seriously at a time when many musicians thought that if you weren't from an Afro-Cuban *barrio* you could never master the idiom. As an American who was fluent in Spanish and had obtained a thorough knowledge of Cuban music, he was comfortable both inside and outside the *barrio*.

For the first time, a new Cuban style originated outside of the island. In fact, it never made much headway in Cuba.[2] When Cuban congueros Mongo Santamaría, Armando Peraza, Patato Valdez and Cándido Camero first heard Afro-Cuban jazz (also called cubop), they were excited by it. All of them quickly found themselves in demand by jazz musicians.

In many respects, Tito Puente took over the development of stateside Cuban music through his arranging prowess and command of the rhythms. Puente developed a style of playing the timbales that was based on rudiments, rolls, paradiddles and other figures associated with snare drumming. Just as he adjusted modern jazz voicings to mesh with Cuban rhythms, he adapted snare techniques to fit into a Cuban timbales style. Puente did not merely change the sound of timbales but of the Cuban rhythm section itself. He developed a stateside version of Cuban rhythms that was faster, harder and louder than homegrown Cuban music. In some respects the rhythm changed for practical reasons: it had "to propel those big saxophone and trumpet sections," as arranger Ray Santos put it.[3]

Puente's music was driven by instrumentals. His music was strongly influenced by mambo, a style in which instrumental forces take center stage. The key aspect of mambo is the antiphonal interchange between instrumental forces. In other words, the trumpets, say, are assigned one choppy passage while the saxophones play a line that zigzags over and between the trumpet melody. With its emphasis on short, often meaningless vocal interjections, it was the perfect style for an audience who didn't speak Spanish. Salsa arrangers maintained mambo's instrumental interplay using small ensembles consisting of a few trumpets and trombones. Nearly all salsa arrangements had a "mambo section" that gave the arranger a chance to work out with his or her jazz skills.

Puente tended to prefer Cuban-style singers whether they were native-born Cubans like Celia Cruz, La Lupe and Rolando La Serie or Puerto Ricans like Chivirico Dávila.[4] But in 1956, he hired Santitos Colón. According to Puente's biographer, the ethnomusicologist Steven Loza, Colón didn't sound like any Cuban singer:

[Colón] did not adhere to what some might refer to as a strict or typical Cuban style of singing in terms of both tonal inflection and the execution of improvised *inspiraciones*. His new, distinctive style was especially marked by a high vocal register and a less strict, sometimes non-rhyming improvisation in which he did not implement some of the more traditional *copla* poetic forms, which Cuban soneros had tended to retain in both innovative and traditional streams.[5]

The most influential of all Puerto Rican-style singers was Ismael "Maelo" Rivera, whose appearances beginning in the late 1950s with the band of Cortijo electrified audiences both in the Caribbean and the United States. The so-called *riveristas*, a group of Puerto Ricans and Nuyoricans headed by Cheo Feliciano and Hector Lavoe, had a different style of singing than the Cuban-style soneros. Willie Colón describes Rivera, his favorite sonero, as follows: "The champ is Ismael Rivera, who practically invented the poly-rhythmic syncopated counterpoint style with double entendre and a great sense of humor."[6]

In the 1960s, stateside Cuban music went through new changes that further consolidated its differences with homegrown Cuban music. A few seemed significant at the time, but proved short-lived. Bugalú, a style that used English lyrics and a rhythm-and-blues influenced beat, was very popular but Puente and other trendsetters disliked it, and it quickly disappeared. What came to prominence was a surprise: a revivalist movement. The rough-and-tough Afro-Cuban music of Arsenio Rodríguez, Miguelito Cuní and Felix Chapotín struck a chord in Puerto Rican neighborhoods. It was a music that unhesitatingly embraced humble roots and, as such, served as a locus of identity for Latinos in much the same way that soul music had functioned for African Americans. The tough sound of *son conjunto* made a perfect fit with the bad-boy image of Latin gangs that a number of future salsa musicians belonged to.

The leaders who succeeded in making *son conjunto* fashionable were Ray Barretto, Eddie Palmieri, Johnny Pacheco and Larry Harlow. None were Cuban: Palmieri and Barretto are Nuyoricans; Pacheco, Dominican and Larry Harlow is Jewish American. Pacheco's inspiration was Felix Chapotín, while Palmieri and Harlow reached far into Arsenio Rodríguez's song catalog. Of these three bandleaders, Pacheco stuck the closest to a pure Cuban sound. Although it wasn't an innovative approach, Pacheco succeeded in creating an appealing, personal style. At times, Harlow enjoyed playing in an authentic Cuban manner. He was one of the few American pianists who could play in the style of prerevolutionary pianists like Peruchín and, especially, Lilín Martínez Griñan, who played piano and wrote songs and arrangements for both Arsenio Rodríguez and Chapotín. Palmieri was from the beginning of his career an original piano stylist, who amalgamated a strong sense of clave with the quartal harmony of McCoy Tyner and the percussive approach of Horace Silver.

Unlike Pacheco, Larry Harlow and Eddie Palmieri were forward-thinking innovative artists. Along with their colleagues, they sought out songwriters like Tito Curet Alonzo and Ruben Blades who could write songs with themes that their largely Puerto Rican audiences could identify with. To the dismay of a few Cuban diehards, they mixed in jazz harmonies together with the old *son conjunto* sound.

Despite the innovations in stateside Cuban music that occurred during the late 1960s and throughout the 1970s, salsa remained in some important ways a revivalist movement. Regardless of what was laid on top of the rhythm, percussionists continued being faithful to the rhythmic traditions of an earlier Cuban generation at a time when homegrown Cuban music had progressed. The arrangements adhered to the old formula: start with the song section (also called *la guía*), next, the *coro* section in which a lead singer sings a few lines of improvised text (known as *la inspiración*) followed by a choral statement. The *coro* and the lead singer exchange back and forth in perpetual dialogue. Next, there might be an instrumental solo improvisation and a written instrumental passage.

The musicians in New York, the heart of salsa, were devoted to staying with a style that their contemporaries on Cuban soil considered outmoded. Although in other respects the salseros were a creative and innovative crowd, when it came to rhythm they were conservative and provincial. In their way of thinking, valid rhythmic innovations had to come from Cuba.

The Cuban Americans in Miami during these years were consumed with nostalgia. They loved the sentimental stylings of Cuban artists such as Los Matamoros and José Antonio María Romeu. They did not especially care for harder fare performed by, and for, Afro-Cubans. As a result, salsa did not find many fans in the early years of the Cuban exile community.

During the 1960s and 1970s, a rumor spread throughout the Latin community that Castro had banished Cuban popular music. The rumor was given a boost by one of the most popular songs in Miami in the 1960s, *El son se fue de Cuba* ("*El son* has left Cuba"). The lyrics speak from an exile's point of view about a *guajira* (country person) who arrives in Havana to find that *el son* has left the country. The song was not written by a Cuban; its author is Billo Frometá, who was from the Dominican Republic. Other ironies abound in this peculiar document that captures the feelings of the early Cuban exile community. The song oozes nostalgia for a genre that, as I already mentioned, had few supporters in Miami. In fact, one was far more likely to hear *el son* in Cuba, where Beny Moré, considered the greatest sonero of all time, resided until his death in 1963. During the 1960s, record stores in Miami refused to carry the albums of any artists who still lived on the island. As a result, it was almost impossible to find Moré's records or albums by artists that paid him tribute.[7]

Nostalgia and musical conservatism are not unknown to Latin American countries. In Mexico, you can hear 60-year-old recordings blasting from a bus driven by a 20 year old. Mexican bands may play the latest hit from the United States and then follow it with a mariachi song from the soundtrack to a 1940s Mexican movie. But in Cuba, old music curries little interest. "What people in Cuba are not listening to is precisely the older music," says Juan Formell, leader of the band Los Van Van.[8]

Salsa eventually proved to be a strong influence on Cuban musicians, who added trombones to their bands in imitation of salsa groups and were inspired by salsa arrangers' use of jazz harmonies. But at first it was greeted with a yawn. Daniel Ponce, a Cuban conguero who immigrated during the *Mariel* boat lift, expressed only the barest respect for music that salsa fans considered *de la onda, muy chevere*. Salseros were good musicians, he stated in a 1985 interview, but hopelessly out of date: "When the Cubans arrived in New York, they all said 'Yuk! This is old music!' I was expecting to find a stronger Latin scene here; the lyrics, the composition, the feeling are not adventurous."[9]

The Cuban people are by no means averse to preserving their traditions, however. There are several thriving folkloric groups, and EGREM (Enterprise of Recordings and Musical Editions) has recorded several historical compilations. But in the arena of popular music, efforts to incorporate the music of the past have failed to attract a broad audience. In the 1970s, Ivory Coast record producer Raoul Diomandé approached EGREM with the idea of a Cuban All-Star group that could compete worldwide with the Fania All-Stars. Areito was the name of EGREM's subsidiary, and the group formed and directed by Juan Pablo Torres was called Las Estrellas de Areito ("The Areito All-Stars"). The group featured musicians who had their heyday before Castro and a few younger musicians, such as Arturo Sandoval, Paquito D'Rivera and Torres himself. The record quickly disappeared. The Cuban people were simply not interested in prerevolutionary music, and the recording got little airplay. Only recently has it resurfaced in the United States, following the immense popularity of the Buena Vista Social Club and its spin-off recordings. In fact, several of the Buena Vista musicians appeared on the Estrellas de Areito recording.

The story of the Buena Vista Social Club is well known, and does not bear repeating in depth. The short version is as follows: Ry Cooder collected a bunch of mostly old Cuban musicians at EGREM's studio under serendipitous circumstances. The group of musicians named itself after a Black social club that was in existence until the early 1960s, when Castro banned all race-based organizations.[10] The music caught on throughout the world. The group has enjoyed sold-out performances at the most prestigious concert halls in the world, phenomenal record sales and a successful movie by Wim Wenders. Soon after the recording came out, there were spin-off recordings by members of the ensemble that also have done well. The financial aspects of the Buena Vista Social Club are a hot topic over the Internet. By U.S. standards, the musicians were not paid a great deal of money. On the other hand, several of them had given up on their musical careers years ago; the recording represented a second chance, one totally unexpected. Many fans believe that the Cuban government only gives the musicians their *per diem* expenses. If this is the case, Castro could correctly respond that Cuban musicians are members of a system devoted to the common good, not to creating millionaires. Before their success, several of the musicians were no longer making an income, but were being provided for by the government.[11]

The Miami Cubans, who usually can be predicted to despise anything coming out of the island, loved the Buena Vista Social Club movie. Latin music critic Judy Cantor of the weekly *Miami New Times* noted that "One of the big reasons it's OK [for exiles] to listen is that it's pre-revolutionary music, not the music of today's Cuba."[12] When the same movie was seen in Cuba, the audience loved seeing their neighborhoods and its inhabitants. They liked the music—who wouldn't be attracted by the charm and expertise of these master musicians? But Cuban tastes in the realm of popular music are progressive. Old Cuban music remains "for export only."

RECENT CUBAN INFLUENCES

In 1969, Cuban arranger, songwriter and bassist Juan Formell formed his own group, Los Van Van. Los Van Van has been the longest-lived popular band since the revolution and the most influential. Formell began with a charanga (Cuban percussion, piano, bass, singers and strings). Then he added a trombone section, giving the group a New York salsa toughness that was relatively new on Cuban soil. Next came the synthesizers and drum machines. In recent years, Formell has followed the lead of American jazz musicians by cutting back on the electronics. Although the instrumentation gave Los Van Van a distinct sound, it was the group's new rhythm, songo, that really pulled people's ears. Formell devised songo with his percussionist, Changuito (José Luis Quintana). Songo was really not just a single rhythm but a whole new orientation toward the Cuban percussion section. In the early years of songo, the bongos disappeared. The conga part was more elaborate and prominent than the one that had become the conguero's staple: the simple figure known as *tumbao*. The conga's partner was at first a souped-up timbale set: the traditional timbale set supplemented by a bass drum. Eventually, the timbales were taken away, and a jazz drum kit moved into the rhythm section. Rumba replaced *el son* as the rhythmic scaffold that held everything together. The bass lines in the popular styles that preceded songo fell into a series of variants: a calypso-like line used in the guaracha and the cha cha, or the so-called "anticipated bass" in which chord tones are anticipated, landing a beat early on 4 rather than on 1. Songo bass lines are considerably freer.

Pianist César Pedroso, co-founder of Los Van Van, helped develop a new style of *guajeo*, the term for the rhythmic piano accompaniment used in Afro-Cuban music. The new style has two characteristics that distinguish it from its predecessors: fewer blank spots and less use of octaves between the hands. In essence, the new Cuban pianist filled in the blank spots between the choppy interjections that typify Latin piano playing. They simply copied the old lines and filled in all the rests. The result is a dense part of almost continuous eighth notes. In the typical *guajeo*, the pianist duplicates two octaves below whatever the right hand is playing. In the new style, the left hand may be playing a line that runs in contrary motion to the right-hand line.

Throughout his career, Formell has been attracted to the latest Cuban expressions. Choosing *Van Van* proved perilous, as he explained in a recent interview with the Columbian Silvana Paternostro:

Really this is the story I tell about our name. In Cuba in the late 60s, at the time of the 1969 sugar harvest, the government was trying to produce ten million tons of sugar and it came up with a slogan: *Los diez millones de que van . . . van* ("The 10 million must go . . . go.") Our name had nothing to do with that. It was just a coincidence, a phrase that was fashionable then. Nothing more. And there's nothing else, no other story. *Van van* in Spanish means it will happen, it will go. It was very hard at that time to get the musicians we wanted to get. One lived in Pinar del Rio. Another one was in another orquesta. . . . I don't know. Each time we would spend a week, two weeks, waiting for a musician so not to get discouraged, we would always say, "¡va, esto va, y de que van van!" That's how we ended up being Los Van Van. But every time I tell the story it ends up being as if Fidel Castro made us call ourselves that. And that is a very ugly story because I don't even know Fidel Castro personally and I don't know if he likes my orquesta and on the contrary, it took a lot of work to get started. No one made me do anything.[13]

Los Van Van has had a difficult time performing in the United States because of its name alone. The Cuban-American community refuses to dis-associate the group's name from the revolutionary slogan. Formell's efforts to distance himself from Castro are understandable in the present political climate in which Fidel has lost nearly all the goodwill he ever had developed on the island and abroad among the left-wing intelligentsia. But he is stretching the truth. His band has always been considered the official group of the Cuban government. Indeed, it could not have achieved its vast popularity on the island without official sanction.

Partly because of its association with Los Van Van, songo did not transplant well in the United States. Another problem is that people did not know how to dance to it. Songo found its way into the hearts of progressive salseros who were intrigued by the latest music from the island. Unlike many of their peers, they did not reject out of hand music coming out of the Cuban Revolution. They realized that songo was a new genre with fascinating new developments in the way Afro-Cuban music was structured. A few of these bands had the rare satisfaction of hearing their compositions recorded by Cuban bands.

Puerto Rican musicians were perhaps a bit more receptive to the new genre than stateside musicians. One of the most famous new songo groups in Puerto Rico was Batacumbele. The group, led by percussionist Ángel "Cachete" Maldonado, was home for a new generation of young Latin musicians like trombone virtuoso Papo Vásquez, trumpeter Charlie Sepúlveda and conguero Giovanni Hidalgo. Batacumbele's lineup included established names such as flutist Nestor Torres, saxophonist Mario Rivera and bassist Eddie "Gua Gua" Rivera. The drumset chair was occupied by *Mariel* exile, Ignacio Berroa. Its most famous song, *Se le ve*, was recorded in Cuba by flutist Richard Egües.

Ruben Blades formed a new group in 1982 with pianist Oscar Hernández as musical director. The accompanying band has at times recorded under its own name, Seis del Solar—"Six from the Ghetto" is a loose translation. Rather than using a traditional salsa rhythm section, Seis del Solar used timbales and a drumset. Robbie Ameen, the group's drummer, was well conversant with songo, and the new rhythm entered into Blades's new songs. In the 1980s, Los Van Van recorded Ruben Blades' *Tierra Dura*.

When the history of Afro-Cuban music is written 25 years from now, its author will propably consider songo a transitional genre, important for evolving into timba. Formell and Los Van Van remained a force in Cuban music by staying in step with the new genre and then rising to the fore as one of its architects and major proponents.

Timba began in the late 1980s. Its seeds were planted when two former Irakere members, tenor saxophonist Carlos Averhoff and flutist José Luis Cortés, formed the group Todos Estrellas in 1986. Also in that group were two future Latin jazz stars, pianist Gonzalo Rubalcaba and drummer Horacio "El Negro" Hernández. A few years later the nucleus of Todos Estrellas became NG La Banda, with José Luis Cortés as its leader. The NG in the band's name stands for *nueva generación*, but its full name is never used. NG La Banda quickly became known as one of the most exciting things to happen in Cuban popular music: fantastic singing, intriguing slang and a virtuoso horn section whose nickname was "the Terror Brass." NG La Banda was loud and extremely aggressive, in the spirit of the nickname its leader goes by: *El Tosco* (the Uncouth One).

Timba singers have tough voices, 360 degrees from the warm syrupy mellifluousness of the Cuban vocal tradition as exemplified in today's Latin music world by Celia Cruz and Ibrahim Ferrer. The lyrics are structured around a lot of group singing, almost in a chorus and refrain pattern, a departure from the format of earlier arrangements. The lyrics, based on the latest popular idioms, lend themselves to gestural interpretations that Cuban audiences join in on.

Timba required a new dance style, at the same time that Cuban audiences demanded a new style of music. Just as timba came into being, the dance known as tembleque also sprung up. It remains a chicken-or-egg quandary which came first, timba or tembleque. While dancers in the United States haven't learned the tembleque, and consequently don't know what to do with timba, timba and the tembleque have spread effortlessly to Italy and Scandinavia.[14]

A few musicians associated with timba have trickled into the United States in the last few years. At least two musicians associated with NG La Banda have defected: saxophonist/arranger Carlos Averhoff and conguero Juan Nogueras. One of the most surprising cases in the annals of Cuban defection is Juan-Carlos Formell, the son of timba musician Juan Formell. The son, a bassist, guitarist and singer, never had much contact with his father. He did not grow up under his father's roof; he was raised by his paternal grandparents. He never played in Los Van Van, either, unlike his brother Samuel Formell, its current drummer. In any case, Juan-Carlos has little interest in timba, and his own music is in a folk-rock style with Afro-Cuban tinges.

So far, timba has not had a discernible effect on stateside Latin music. The current wisdom is that, because of its extensive slang vocabulary, it has no future outside Cuba. While it is true that other Latinos may not be able to understand all the words, this is not a de facto deterrent to a music's popularity away from its native soil. American popular music provides numerous examples of styles that have gained rapid acceptance even though no one understands the words. Country blues is a perfect example. A more recent example is rap, whose words don't mean much unless you know the current ghetto slang.

It is foreseeable that timba will sprout in the United States in the next few years. Recent defectors to the music are dedicated followers. They made up the majority of NG La Banda's audience when the group performed in Miami in November 1999.[15] Audiences at New York City club SOB's were filled with enthusiastic fans from what appeared to be a worldwide Spanish-speaking audience that knew the respective repertoires of these bands. Juan Formell recently won a Grammy award. It seems inevitable that some of this enthusiasm for timba will rub off on stateside Cuban musicians who realize that, although Buena Vista Social Club's music is beautiful, it does not speak to today's world the same way that timba does.

2

Afro-Cuban Musicians in the United States

The U.S. branch of Afro-Cuban musicians begins with Mario Bauzá. Although a few Cuban musicians came before him (flutist Albert Socarrás, singer Antonio Machín), it was Bauzá who initiated an entirely new form of Cuban music that I have dubbed "stateside Cuban music."

Mario Bauzá's upbringing was as unique as the music he created after he emigrated to the United States.[1] Bauzá was born in Havana in 1911, one of six children born to Hilario and Dolores Bauzá. His godparents were wealthy Cubans who, because they were childless, asked Mario's parents if they could raise the child as their own son. As a result, Bauzá got an extensive education in classical music. His first instrument was the clarinet. He went to New York for the first time when he was 15 as a member of the Antonio María Romeu Orchestra. While there, he bought an alto saxophone and quickly learned it. When he got back to Cuba, Bauzá announced to his girlfriend, Stella Grillo, that he would soon return to New York for good. In 1930, he went back to New York to make a career as a musician. Bauzá played with African American swing bands and Latin bands. To increase his marketability as a musician, Bauzá took up the trumpet. In 1936, Bauzá returned to Cuba to marry Stella Grillo, whose brother, Francisco, was a singer with the nickname Machito. Two years later, Bauzá got Machito to join him in New York. In 1940, they formed Machito and the Afro-Cubans, a cross between an American swing band and a Latin group that became the stateside home of Afro-Cuban music. Bauzá helped arriving Afro-Cuban musicians get jobs, and continued to do so for several decades. In the early 1940s, singer Marcelino Guerra, composer of the famous songs, *Pare Cochero* and *A Mi Manera*, came to New York. Bauzá and Machito set the singer up with a group to perform whenever Machito and the Afro-Cubans were unavailable. The Second Afro-Cubans, as the orchestra was known, performed Machito's arrangements.[2] In 1947, percussionist Chano Pozo came to New York to do some recordings that also included members of the Machito orchestra. Bauzá recommended Pozo to Dizzy Gillespie. It was the beginning of a famous collaboration that had a profound effect on the development of Latin jazz. Nearly 40 years later, Bauzá sent Cuban jazz drummer Ignacio Berroa to Dizzy Gillespie. The Cuban drummer stayed with Gillespie for several years. Tito Puente, who began his career as a percussionist in Machito and the Afro-Cubans, followed in Bauzá's footsteps by fostering the talents of Cuban musicians from Mongo Santamaría to, most recently, Juan Pablo Torres.

Being an Afro-Cuban was somewhat of a novelty in the jazz world of the 1920s and 1930s. When Bauzá was a member of the Cab Calloway band, the leader called him "Indian"—short for West Indian. But the small Afro-Cuban community in the northeast was beginning to grow. In the 1930s, there were established centers of Cuban cigar-making in New York and Philadelphia that were swelling with newly arrived Afro-Cuban cigar workers who came up north after 1930, when the Florida cigar industry collapsed.

Afro-Cubans had begun coming to the United States in the nineteenth century. Most of the first Afro-Cuban immigrants were cigar workers who came to Tampa, Florida, to work in cigar factories owned by Cubans and Spaniards.[3] They lived in the towns of West Tampa and Ybor City. Afro-Cubans constituted a minority of the workers, who in addition to white Cubans included Spaniards, Italians, southerners and American Blacks. The Cuban workers were passionately involved in Cuban politics, and many tithed their income to supply funds for Cuban revolutionaries. The economic turmoil following Cuban independence stranded Afro-Cubans, dashing their plans to immediately return to the island for good. Soon after, Afro-Cubans found their situations worsening as racist policies were made into law.

Within the Cuban immigrant community, Afro-Cubans found an escape from the harsh realities of the Jim Crow South. They founded a social club and mutual aid society called La Union Martí-Maceo. Antonio Maceo was the Afro-Cuban general who fought for Cuban independence; José Martí was a writer who inspired several generations of Cuban revolutionaries. La Union Martí-Maceo sponsored concerts, plays, dances and a baseball team, the Cuban Giants (Los Gigantes Cubanos). There were music lessons for children and classes in Spanish.

When the Jim Crow era began, relations between white and Black Cubans soured, following the pattern set by the larger society. But, in general, segregation laws were laxly enforced and friendships across the color line continued to develop. While Jim Crow laws may have lumped Afro-Cubans with Black Americans, social constraints prevented Afro-Cubans from fully assimilating into African American culture. In addition to the language barrier, religious differences kept the two groups apart. The majority of Afro-Cubans were Catholic, and sent their children to largely Cuban parochial schools, while nearly all African Americans in the Tampa area were Protestants. Afro-Cubans discouraged their children from marrying African Americans. No love was lost on the part of African Americans, who were hostile to Afro-Cubans, calling them "black wops."

The vast majority of Afro-Cubans traveled back and forth between Tampa and Cuba, taking advantage of inexpensive steamboat travel. Those who decided to return to Cuba were quickly replaced by new Afro-Cuban workers. Census studies indicate that the overall dimensions of the Afro-Cuban community remained largely the same. The steady travel back to the island as well as the replacement of Afro-Cubans returning to the island tended to reinforce a sense of Cuban identity in the community that persisted until 1930, when the Florida cigar industry took a dive that it never recovered from.

The building that housed the social club became a favorite for concert promoters who rented the hall for African American audiences and hired performers such as Cab Calloway and Chick Webb. By 1960, the Afro-Cuban community in the Tampa area was reduced, and the young generation of Afro-Cubans assimilated into the broader African American culture. As white cigar workers moved away, their houses were bought by African Americans, so neighborhoods that had formerly been Cuban and biracial became solidly black and predominantly American.

After 1930, Tampa was no longer the locus of Afro-Cubans in the United States. In urban centers up north Afro-Cubans were nearly invisible in Cuban neighborhoods, which were primarily white. Afro-Cuban music developed its stateside home not in Cuban neighborhoods, which outside of Tampa were primarily white, but in Puerto Rican neighborhoods, where Afro-Cubans mixed with dark-skinned Puerto Ricans. As the number of Afro-Cuban musicians climbed, the immigration of Afro-Cubans in general declined steadily. After the 1959 Cuban Revolution, the number of Afro-Cuban immigrants dropped enormously. Only 5% of Cuban immigrants were Afro-Cubans. Today, Little Havana, the home of the Cuban refugee population, is over 99% white.

One of the main reasons why Afro-Cuban musicians left Cuba was racism. Although they could work in music, they were not able to thrive. They saw the United States as the land of opportunity in which Louis Armstrong, Cab Calloway and Duke Ellington had surmounted racism to gain financial success and respect. The fact that these musicians expressed themselves through the medium of jazz was significant to Afro-Cuban musicians. Mongo Santamaría, Armando Peraza, Patato Valdez and Cándido Camero began their careers in the United States playing in Latin groups but soon found their way to spots in jazz groups, where they got better pay and were treated with more respect. The jazz world regarded them as exotic stars, rather than background figures in a rhythm section.

The United States had a strong effect on Cuban racism after American forces began occupying Cuban soil. American officials' lack of respect for Cuba's Afro-Cuban soldiers lowered their status in Cuban society. The spending power of American tourists pushed the Cuban tourist industry to cater to American sensibilities and to deny Blacks access to hotels and beaches. Rich Cubans who were educated in the South took back to Cuba the racist attitudes they learned there. But Cuban racism was by no means a carbon copy of that of its North American neighbor.

Cuba had a more complex form of racism than the simpler polar model of the United States, where bigoted whites tended to treat all people of African descent equally poorly, regardless of their skin tone and background. By 1950, Antonio Maceo was a national hero, and many upper-class Cubans had family members with a touch of African blood. Cuban racism could be incredibly ironic when it came to politics. Fulgencio Batista, the strong-arm general who brought about his own downfall, was apparently a mulatto. He surrounded himself with Afro-Cuban henchmen and was rumored to be a follower of Santería. Fidel Castro, who stepped into the vacuum created when Batista, cut off from his own army, fled the country, is a white man from a well-off Christian family. Few of his early comrades were Black, although Castro saw himself as the savior of Afro-Cubans and worked to alleviate conditions in Afro-Cuban neighborhoods.

In some respects, Cubans are more jocular about race than Americans in the United States. Cubans of all colors seem to enjoy songs with lyrics that African Americans would cringe at. For example, consider two songs made famous by Cachao (Israel Cachao López) and Celia Cruz that poke fun at big-lipped dark-skinned Cubans without a trace of irony: Cachao's descarga tune, *Cuchara e' Bembe* ("Spoon-lips") and Celia Cruz's *Bemba Colorao* ("Colored African Lips").

Thousands of Cuban songs use racial terminology. To an outsider, it is tempting to find significance in all the *negras, prietos, chinitas* and *morenos* in Cuban song lyrics. But, in fact, racial terminology has become ingrained in Cuban Spanish—as it has in Puerto Rican Spanish and Brazilian Portuguese,[4] for that matter—with a descriptive ease that is untranslatable. *Mi negra*, while literally meaning "my black woman," is used colloquially as the equivalent of "my old lady." *Negrita* certainly means something like "my black girl" but it may be the affectionate equivalent of "honey." *Mi china* means "my Chinese girl," but the person being described could also be very dark with heavy-lidded eyes.[5]

In Cuba, the recognition that African culture has been a powerful influence came earlier and, in some ways, with fewer difficulties than in the United States, where there is a strong tradition of crediting whites for African American creations and a tendency to concentrate on the negative side of African American society. From the seeds planted by the *Afrocubanismo* movement developed by Cuban writers and musicians in the 1920s has grown the belief, now subscribed to by Cubans of all stripes, that African-influenced music and religion is the natural inheritance of all Cubans, whether or not their skin is dark or they were born in a *solar*. Cuban expression and Afro-Cuban expression have, in fact, become nearly synonymous.[6]

In the post-World War II period, Afro-Cubans found that the racial climate was changing in their favor. Ironically, in part this was a result of the North American influx of tourists. While pre-World War II white Cubans favored their government's policies of marginalizing Afro-Cuban culture, it was American tourists who helped bring it back. They flocked to nightclub acts in which rumba and Afro-Cuban street culture were the featured attraction. The comparsa, the Cuban carnival banned because it inspired disreputable behavior, returned when officials realized that tourists would flock to the annual event. Dark-skinned singing stars like Celia Cruz and Beny Moré were finding it easier to achieve success. A Cuban American friend of mine remembers seeing Celia Cruz on television. It was the mid-1950s, a period when there were virtually no Black faces on U.S. television channels. As 1995 Cuban exile Evaristo M. Martínez-Martínez explains, "Whenever you see a group of blacks and whites mingling very well, you can suspect they are Cubans. I think that this is part of our diet—white rice and black beans together. All this did not happen because of Castro. [You can] find in Cuba's history the name of José Martí, Antonio Maceo, Máximo Gomez, Mariana Grajales, and many others."[7]

By the time Cuban race relations were improving, Cándido, Armando Peraza and Mongo Santamaría had already departed Cuba for good, frustrated with being left behind artistically and financially.

Afro-Cuban musicians discovered that the Jim Crow laws and social mores of the United States had some unforeseen benefits. Unlike in Cuba, lighter skin did not confer any special legal privileges. As a result, light-skinned African Americans were ready to accept their brotherhood with other people of African descent. Armando Peraza noted: "The African-American mulatto here in the United States says, 'I'm black.' In the Latin community it's not like that. They want to pass. And they'll tell you, 'No, no, no. Me, African? No, no, no.' "

Then there were the negative effects of race. The racial climate in the United States acted to form a wedge among Latin musicians based on color. Mario Bauzá noted with sadness that, in the 1930s, Latin white musicians banded together to improve their lot, while tolerating "the exclusion of dark-skinned Latin musicians from their Broadway bands."[8] Bauzá and

Machito's most revolutionary act was to form under the banner "Afro-Cuban" an orchestra that was mixed both racially and ethnically.[9]

After the Cuban Revolution the ranks of white Cubans living in the United States swelled to numbers that no one could have imagined. They quickly got a reputation for being racially intolerant. However, Marty Sheller remembers that during the 1960s white Cuban refugees would come backstage to congratulate Santamaría on his successful career, but the conga player was uncomfortable with these encounters. As an Afro-Cuban musician, he simply didn't trust white Cuban American strangers. "As far as they're concerned," Santamaría told *Downbeat* journalist Arnold Jay Smith, "it was the 'nigger who drinks, chews tobacco and plays.' "[10]

3

The Cuban Revolution

Cuban musicians who left in the years before the Cuban Revolution typically profess disinterest in Cuban politics. The reasons are simple: (1) they
may still have relatives living on the island and don't want to jeopardize
their lives or (2) they are tired of getting into heated political discussions.
As a result, when questioned about Cuba, their responses may border on
the disingenuous. For example, Chocolate Armenteros told Rick Davies
that the politics of the Cuban Revolution had little to do with his decision
to immigrate. It seems hard to believe.

Although Mongo Santamaría dislikes many of Castro's policies, he believes that through his ambitious public works projects the Cuban leader
has improved the lives of Afro-Cubans.[1] Santamaría asserted that Castro
had solved the race problem nearly entirely, a view that is also the official
position of the Cuban government.[2] To further the process of eradicating
racial perspectives, Castro abolished all social organizations based on race,
such as the Buena Vista Social Club that the famed Cuban group named
itself after. In fact, it has not been until the last decade that Cuban intel-
lectuals like Gisela Arandia Covarrubia have received official permission to
study the lives of Afro-Cubans from a racial perspective. In truth, the racial
problem has continued to persist long after the revolution. One Cuban
refugee, who arrived in the United States in 1989, notes that in his high
school, out of a student body of 1,000, there were two mulattoes and one
black.[3]

It is a wonder that Santamaría is so evenhanded in his consideration of
the Cuban government. In 1976, the Cuban government denied him per-

mission to visit his mother when she was dying. They had no cause to be hostile toward him. Unlike those who arrived after the revolution, Santamaría could properly be categorized as an immigrant, rather than a refugee. He had left Cuba before anyone had heard of Fidel Castro. One could understand why *el Comandante* might be angry with *los gusanos*—the "worms," his term for Cubans who chose to avoid what he considered the noble cause of throwing in their lot with the common good in exchange for a better life in a capitalist society. But there was no reason except spite at the success Santamaría had achieved in the United States for keeping the musician away from his mother, whom he had not seen for 16 years. The only way he was able to finally travel to the island was through singer Miriam Makeba's intercession at the United Nations, where she secured him a visa. Soon after the visit, Santamaría's mother passed away.[4]

Celia Cruz is one of the few prominent musicians of Santamaría's generation with a strong political agenda: she is virulently anti-Castro. Cruz has recorded dozens of songs that express her undying love for the island. She made headlines in the Latin American news media when she condemned Puerto Rican singer Andy Montañez for hugging Silvio Rodríguez, a Cuban singer who writes protest songs inspired by the Cuban Revolution. Subsequently, she canceled her performance at the First International Festival of Salsa in Puerto Rico to avoid a boycott by Puerto Ricans angered by her snubbing Montañez.

Musicians who escaped Cuba since the *Mariel* boat lift share Celia Cruz's strong hatred of Castro. While some of the defectors were not well known in Cuba, others had achieved the top status available to Cuban artists on the island. They defected because they hated living under communism, not simply to find opportunities unavailable to them in Cuba.

In 1980, drummer Ignacio Berroa took advantage of the 1980 *Mariel* boat lift to escape to the United States. "The decision was simple. I left Cuba looking for freedom, not just artistic freedom." He came from an Afro-Cuban family who, in the early years of the revolution, were fervent followers of Castro. The family began changing their minds after an uncle was arrested for corruption charges. Berroa's family was amazed by the uncle's horrific tales of mistreatment. When Berroa was a young music student, he was repeatedly sent to the police station for carrying around recordings of American artists he loved such as Dizzy Gillespie, the Beatles and the Rolling Stones. Like other Cubans, Berroa was angered by the new forms of discrimination developed by the Castro government: he was sent away from hotels and beaches reserved for party members and foreigners and advised not to mix with tourists. He was angered by being underpaid for his work. After graduating from a Cuban conservatory, he was assigned an unpaid teaching position at the García Caturla conservatory. When he performed in Spain with the group Experimentación Sonora del ICAI before crowds of 2,500 people who paid an $8 admission charge, he was paid $8 per day.

Although Berroa was glad to leave Cuba, he came with ideas indoctrinated into all Cuban citizens by their government about the poor state of racial relations in the United States. He feared he would never be able to play drums again and would have to wash floors or clean dishes for the rest of his life. Fortunately, his fears proved groundless. Six weeks after arriving in New York, an acquaintance of his father, violinist Ignacio Berroa, Sr., asked him to play on a record date. From then on, Berroa was in constant demand. His artistic talent was recognized for the first time in his life.

While his musical career thrived, Berroa's personal life was in disarray. Until he managed to apply pressure on the Cuban government, his wife and son were held hostage for four-and-a-half years.

Berroa is extremely aware that outside of the Cuban exile community, Castro is regarded as a colorful and heroic figure, a champion to Cuba's poor and its Afro-Cuban population. In Berroa's opinion, Castro gets away with his lies because "unfortunately, this man has an incredible charisma; he's an incredible actor."

Saxophonist Paquito D'Rivera came to the United States a year after Berroa. Unlike Berroa, he was already an international star, one of the best-paid musicians under Cuban communism. D'Rivera played in the jazz group Irakere. Jesús "Chucho" Valdés and D'Rivera were the musical directors of the group. Valdés chose the name "Irakere," a Yoruba word meaning "forest" or "jungle," partly as a ruse to prevent officials from being aware that the musicians were dedicated to jazz.[5]

Irakere was the first group since the revolution to be given permission by the U.S. government to perform here. The group's appearances at the Newport and Montreux jazz festivals in 1978 were a sensation. Its subsequent U.S. recordings sold well and received critical acclaim. The members of Irakere reached a level of success and official recognition shared by only the most well-off Cuban artists. Irakere's success made it possible for jazz musicians to play on the island freely for the first time since Castro seized power, without fear of being accused of spreading pro-Yankee, counter-revolutionary tendencies.

D'Rivera believes that music has flourished during Castro's regime "despite, and not thanks to," Castro. The Cuban leader has "destroyed the Cuban people mentally and made them become liars who cannot risk telling what they really think about Castro. Even a spokesman for the socialist system, [nueva trova singer] Pablo Milanés, has acknowledged to me privately that he feels himself being censured. And the truth is that, wherever the Cuban Revolution has passed, the grass no longer grows."[6]

As when Berroa fled Cuba, Castro made D'Rivera's family suffer for his defection. It took D'Rivera eight years before he was able to get his son to rejoin him in the United States. Anyone who seeks to interpret Castro's efforts to return Elián González to his father as a result of simple human kindness should be reminded of D'Rivera's hardships.

Arturo Sandoval was Paquito D'Rivera's partner in Irakere. Sandoval took another approach to leaving Cuba, at least on temporary jaunts across the world: he joined the Communist Party. The trumpeter had no sympathy for the Cuban government whatsoever. Joining the party was nothing more than a means to avoid official criticism and, more important, keep from being disconnected from his family. Party members were allowed to bring their family on trips. Besides enjoying their company, Sandoval didn't have to worry about what would happen to them during his absences.

Sometimes what appears to be the best plan of action in a difficult situation ends up backfiring. When Sandoval finally defected in the early 1990s, he was first welcomed into the United States. But when the American government discovered that Sandoval was a party member, he was denied refugee status. At first, it appeared that the Immigration and Naturalization Service was simply complying with official policies. It took several years before Sandoval was able to persuade officials that his membership was simply a ploy. Until then, it was a real Catch-22 situation for the multitalented musician, as he told me in a telephone interview: in Cuba he was accused of being pro-Yankee; in the United States, he was accused of being a communist.[7]

Directly after his defection, Sandoval was given superstar treatment. He played at the White House, at the presidential inauguration, at Vice President Gore's private residence and halftime at the Super Bowl. It seemed a sure thing for the famed musician to obtain his citizenship. Somehow, the Miami branch of the INS managed to deny his request. In the ensuing brouhaha, Sandoval's case was reviewed. They found that his testimony had been twisted and his file was missing important documents. Subsequently, Sandoval testified once again, this time in front of a video camera and a court reporter. Shortly thereafter, in December 1998, Sandoval was granted citizenship. Sandoval was always suspicious that the Cuban government had had their hands in the whole affair. For several months, Sandoval's difficulties in the United States provided Castro with news stories that warned anyone considering defection of being maltreated by the U.S. government.[8] In February 2000, Mariano Faget, a 34-year veteran of the INS, was arrested in Miami for spying on behalf of the Cuban government. Faget was the INS supervisor responsible for overseeing decisions regarding the naturalization of immigrants, including defectors.[9]

Sandoval is impressed by the current success of the Buena Vista Social Club musicians. Although he knows them personally and is fond of them, he does not believe that their music is the best Cuba has to offer. "I've always said, and I'll die saying it: if you want to hear the most authentic

Cuban music, you don't have to go to Cuba and find the Buena Vista Social Club. Just listen to a Celia Cruz record."[10] Reporter Daniel Chang says that Sandoval "insists that he has not heard anything good come out of Cuba of late." Chang finds that "this sentiment must be taken with a grain of salt because, for Sandoval, any music that comes out of Cuba today must be associated with Castro."[11]

What happened to the rest of Irakere after it lost its horn section? Chucho Valdés simply kept it going, replacing Sandoval and D'Rivera with one virtuoso after another. In the recent thaw in relations between Cuba and the United States, Valdés has been performing steadily in the United States and records for Blue Note Records under his own name. Like other successful Cuban musicians, he spends more time in Europe and the United States than at home. The Cuban government has lifted some of its restrictions on how much income artists are entitled to, and with the dollar being an accepted form of currency and one of the only bright sides in the Cuban economy, Cuban artists are doing much better than they did when Sandoval and D'Rivera were still living there.

Singer Albita Rodríguez goes by her first name alone. Albita, who came from a well-known musical family, was one of the stars of Cuban popular music. She was a familiar face on Cuban television, where she appeared on the weekly show, *Palmas y Cañas*. Her records sold well, and Albita performed throughout the world. In 1991, the singer was offered a recording contract by a Colombian company. She was granted permission to move to Colombia, but the Cuban government continued to collect most of her earnings. In 1993, Albita had had enough of her government's policies. She arranged a recording date at a Mexican studio and then casually walked over the border into the United States along with the members of her group, who have continued to perform with her in the United States. She was enthusiastically greeted by the Cuban American community, who recognized with delight that her defection would be received as a slap on the face by the Castro government. A year later, Albita was signed by Emilio Esteban to his Crescent Moon label, a subsidiary of Epic Records. In the United States, she cut her hair short and died it platinum blond. She took on an androgynous look, and wrote songs about Cuban identity but also dealing with sexual identity. By dealing with these two themes in tandem, Albita gets her Cuban American audience, who strongly respond to her songs about Cuban pride, to at least consider the validity of the other, less mainstream topic:

As the title of her first recording, *No se parece a nada* ("Unlike Anything Else") immediately suggests, Albita is concerned with the experience of foreignness, both her adopted nation's and her own within that nation. The radical cultural reversals that Albita's music performs are at once sexual and political. Her music bears explicit witness to her androgeny as the central, informing component of her curiously patriotic Cubanness.[12]

One of the most unlikely stories about Cuban artists living in the United States is that of Gonzalo Rubalcaba. The Cuban government has permitted this intense young pianist to retain his citizenship but live abroad. First, Rubalcaba resided in Santo Domingo, but since 1996 has made his home in Ft. Lauderdale. It is an option unheard of ten years ago. Because he is not a Cuban defector, Rubalcaba is unwilling to criticize his government, to the dismay of the Cuban American community. When he gave his first performance in Miami, he was denounced in an ugly manner that drew shame on that community. In 1996, he and his family settled in Ft. Lauderdale, where he has feared for his wife and children. "I struggle most with the human issues and family values in America," Rubalcaba said through his manager and interpreter, Juan Quesada. "Life has always moved me wherever I've needed to go, and I feel comfortable [in the States] now. I still have in my heart where I come from, but I don't feel like a stranger here at all."[13]

When Ignacio Berroa performed with Gonzalo Rubalcaba several years ago, he was criticized by the Cuban American community for "playing with a Communist." Now, it would scarcely attract much notice, even for the most right-wing members of the Cuban refugee community. It has been a commonplace event for Cuban defectors to play with Cuban touring musicians. Pianist Alfredo Rodríguez, for many years a French resident, has performed and recorded with Cuban trumpeter Jesús Alemañy. Juan-Carlos Formell and Juan Pablo Torres, musicians who defected from Cuba in the 1990s, have both played with the Buena Vista Social Club.[14] The rule of thumb seems to be that Cubans are welcome to play in the United States, and Cuban defectors may play with them, so long as the Cubans aren't fans of Fidel Castro. In other words, it is permissible to perform with Gonzalo Rubalcaba or Chucho Valdés—but beware associating with nueva trova singers like Silvio Rodríguez or Pablo Milanés and other past and present spokespersons for the revolution.

4

Mongo Santamaría in Cuba

Mongo Santamaría is a short, graceful man full of warmth and charm. He lives in Miami in a condo and in an apartment on Manhattan's West Side, where he has resided for close to 40 years. When I interviewed him, he had recently decided to retire from music due to health problems, some stemming from a bus accident he had nearly a half-century ago. His apartment is very tidy. There are a few statues and wall hangings depicting Yoruba deities and a wooden African drum standing five feet tall. On the wall is a picture of some of his children, of whom he is extremely proud. There are also plenty of CDs, because Santamaría is an avid listener of Cuban, Brazilian and, much to my surprise, Arabic music.

Santamaría has strong opinions about music and keeps up with the latest Cuban sounds. Santamaría is generally free of the envy and jealousy that affect many musicians. He admires Puerto Rican conguero Giovanni Hidalgo, Cuban drummer Horacio "El Negro" Hernández, and Cuban exile Ignacio Berroa, also a drummer. He also spoke with pride about playing on the hit song *Cloud Nine* with drummer Bernard "Pretty" Purdie.

I admire Santamaría, not only because he is a fantastic conguero and bongo player and the person responsible for introducing Afro-Cuban street music to the United States, but because he is an immigrant success story. Like others who began life in poverty in a foreign land, he moved to the United States to find his fortune. But it was his determination to reach an international audience that motivated him.

When I started my band, I started with the idea that I wanted to play for the majority of people; that's what I like. What I like is travelling all over the world and playing for people—Chinese, Hungarian, Jewish, Indian, everybody! Not to play for only a few people. For that matter, I would never have left my country. That's not only for economical reasons. It's so that you're going to be pleased that more people know you and your music. That's the only way.[1]

Although I realized that Santamaría knows English, I thought he would be more comfortable speaking Spanish. Toward the end of the interview, Santamaría switched to English. I am grateful to musician Mossa Bildner for helping me with the interview. Bildner, who is fluent in Spanish as well as several other languages, grew up in Brazil and is well acquainted with its music and Afro-Brazilian religious traditions. Santamaría loves Brazilian culture and has played with many of its leading musicians, so our conversation began with a discussion of Brazilian music. Since Bildner has participated in Brazilian religious traditions that bear many similarities to Cuban practices, she was able to involve Santamaría in a discussion of religious culture that would probably not have been as successful if I had conducted the interview alone.

Santamaría's 40-year career as a bandleader has woven a pattern formed from three continuous threads: Afro-Cuban street music, Afro-Cuban-inflected funk and Latin jazz. The oldest thread in Santamaría's career is Afro-Cuban street music, a connection that came about when he was born, because it was the only music around him when he was a baby.

LIFE IN CUBA

I was born in Cuba, April 7, 1917. In the 40s I worked as a musician and mailman for eight years. I think my nickname Mongo comes from Africa from a people called Mali. Mongo—the chief of the tribe. I lived in the Havana *barrio* called Jesús María. It was about 95% Black, a working-class people who worked on the docks.[2]

Jesús María is a small *barrio* in central Havana that adjoins Los Sitios, a somewhat larger Afro-Cuban *barrio*. Jesús María is also called Amalia.[3] Afro-Cuban lyrics are full of references to Amalia and Amalianos, the residents of Amalia. The singer may tell an "Amaliano" to pay attention to his great music, or he or she sings "Amalia, Amalia, Amalia," just for the flavor of the vocables in the word, not for any other meaning.

My Dad was a construction worker and my mother sold coffee and cigarettes for a long time. My father didn't live with my mother. And then my Dad died when he was 41 and I was just a kid. [I was raised by] my mother, my grandmother, my cousins. We were a large family. I have a brother on my father's side (same father, different mother) who died about five or six years ago in Cuba named Orestes. On my mother's side I have a sister who lives in Miami, my youngest sister. I was the only musician. My grandfather came from the Congo. I knew him when I was very young. I don't remember him very well. When I went to Cuba [a few years ago] my cousin Luis told me about him and told me he was from the Congo.[4]

Santamaría's full name is Ramón Santamaría Rodríguez. His father was Ramón Santamaría Gimenez, and his mother was Felicia Rodríguez Bazan. In some respects, Santamaría had a typical upbringing for a *muchachito del barrio (barrio* boy). Illegitimacy was the rule among Black families, double what it was for whites. Most fathers, like Santamaría's, lived apart from their children, and often contributed nothing to their upbringing.[5] When Black fathers and mothers lived together, it was often a common-law relationship known as *arrimado*. In this type of relationship, the man and woman considered themselves single, although they refer to their lover as "husband" or "wife." In Cuba, unlike other parts of Latin America where marriage was prohibitively expensive for the lower classes, a civil marriage was within the means of most poor Cubans, at a price of $2 to $5. The *arrimado* was thus chosen over civil marriages for purely social reasons.[6] In Cuba's macho culture, men enjoyed the freedom to leave an *arrimado* without having the responsibility of child-care thrust on them—which would have been the case had they been legally married.[7]

Others in Santamaría's generation also had grandparents who had been born in Africa and brought as slaves to Cuba in the final days of legal slavery—before the 1880s. First-generation Africans were called *negros de nación*. A less respectful name for them was *bozales*, the Spanish equivalent of "greenhorn." Their Spanish dialect was imitated in countless songs and comedy routines in Cuba's version of minstrelsy, *el teatro vernáculo* (the vernacular theatre).

My family lived in a *solar*, an inexpensive place with a lot of little rooms. The people paid four or five pesos a month in rent because they didn't have much. They lived there because of discrimination—same problem as in the United States with the Black people, Harlem, Soweto in South Africa. It's the same thing. Like in Washington Heights the lights went off. There are more poor people there and they wanted them to suffer more than others. But there were poor whites who also lived in the *solares*.[8]

Solares, which may loosely be translated as "tenement houses," are usually old buildings that once exclusively housed whites with "a sufficient number of rooms to ensure the owner a good profit."[9] Several *solares* were built to be sanatoriums or hotels, like the *solar* "Miami." The average number of family members sharing a room was 5, and in rooms rented by Afro-Cubans there were sometimes as many as 14. People had to sleep in shifts in these large families, and even with this arrangement of sleep hours the older boys had to stay up all night and sleep during the daytime.

Children in the *solares* played ball, any kind of thing. We went swimming. We took a bus and went to the docks, to the Malecón. We had to be careful about sharks. We went to school and attended church. It's the same thing as here.[10]

In the neighborhood where I came from we had all kinds of music, mostly from Africa. We did not leave it alone; we changed it our way. The music we made dealt with religion and conversation. The drum was our tool and we used it for everything.[11]

Santamaría grew up in a world that was off-limits to all but the poorest Cubans. Masculine bravado was in the air they breathed. Music was mixed into their daily lives, and was imbued with a competitive spirit. Singers engaged each other in verbal jousts, and dancers worked to assert their superiority and originality. Drummers with names like Miguelito Cara Ancho (Broad-faced Mickey) engaged in knife fights.

Close by the living quarters of Santamaría's family was the Jesús María park where Havana's rumberos met along with dockworkers and carpenters. Here he could hear the famous drummer Roberto Izquierdo play *quinto*. The junior rumberos who were 10 or 11 years old met at the corner of Águila and Diaria Streets to practice their drumming and dancing.[12] Every week there was a rumba in front of someone's house. Santamaría and his friends brought their drums to entertain their friends and family members. They sang songs that they had learned or made up on the spot. There would always be partygoers who knew at what point in the lyrics they were expected to sing back the lead singer's words. Meanwhile, a single pair of dancers would be responding to the music. The man would try to "get" the woman with a sudden hand, foot or pelvic thrust known as a *vacunao*—literally, a "vaccination," but really a sexual advance. The woman would respond with a *botao*,[13] an action in which she blocks his movements and keeps from getting "vaccinated." This dance, the guaguancó, was not the only one danced at these parties. And when there was a male dancer around who knew how to execute the complex moves, the drummers would play rumba columbia.[14] When they weren't playing guaguancó, columbia or the slow couple dance called yambú, the musicians along with everybody else at the party were drinking rum. Although the rumbas were usually peaceful neighborhood affairs, at times they would erupt into deadly brawls. The police were often there to crack down on *rumbónes* ("rumba parties"), to maintain the peace or use their presence as an excuse to hassle poor Blacks.

Santamaría learned about Santería practically from birth. His grandmother would take him to the ceremonies when he was six or seven years old. She cooked sacred food for the orishas (deity or spirits). For Chango, for example, there was amalá flour, which was ground by hand, then wrapped in a banana leaf and eaten plain or with sugar. Ochún's food was ochinchín, which was made with watercress, chard, almonds and boiled shrimp. Obatalá had a black-eyed pea stew.[15]

Like many other Afro-Cuban musicians of his generation, Santamaría grew up listening to Lucumí praise chants, the songs sung in the Santería religion. Yoruba is the sacred language of Santería. Lucumí is probably a corrupt version of a Yoruba phrase *Oluku mi*, meaning "my friend."[16] Santamaría knows some Yoruba words, and he told me that his cousin Luis is practically fluent. Like all other drummers, Santamaría's personal orisha is Chango, the god of music. Although he has been a lifelong devotee, he was never initiated. There is nothing unusual about his status in the religion: the participation of non-initiates in Santería is fairly common. Santamaría learned to play for bembes, the music played at religious festivities celebrating the oricha's birthdays and the anniversaries of initiations of Santeros, full-fledged members of the religion. Santamaría told me about the main days on which bembes were organized: El dia del Caridad de Cobre, the patron saint of Cuba, el dia de Oyá (the deity/spirit of graveyards), el dia de Santa Barbara, who is Chango in the Santería religion, and el dia de San Lazaro—Babaluaye in Santería.

As a teenager, Santamaría learned to play the toques de santo, the ritualized greetings addressed to the pantheon of orishas. Traditionally these are performed on batá drums. According to Santamaría, they "weren't used much at that time," probably because musicians were scared that the police would confiscate them, which they had been doing for decades. Although the rumbero *barrios* were fertile ground for Afro-Cuban arts, they still had to be practiced with an eye out for the police. During Santamaría's youth, Santería and African-derived arts in general were forbidden by the authorities. In 1922, President Alfredo Zayas outlawed Afro-Cuban gatherings involving drumming and dance.[17] But, during the 1930s, the hourglass-shaped drums and the music that they played were beginning to be promoted as cultural treasures. In December 1935, the Black scholar Gustavo Urrutia featured the batá on a program that was part of a series of broadcasts on the development of Black economic power.[18] In 1936, Don Fernando Ortiz, the father of Afro-Cuban studies and the man who coined the word *Afro-Cuban*, gave a lecture featuring a famous trio of bataleros led by Pablo Roche. This was the first public performance of batá. Among Roche's living disciples are Francisco Aguabella and Julito Collazo, who immigrated to the United States at around the same time as Santamaría. Aguabella[19] and Collazo[20] were the first bataleros in the United States and remain among the few drummers in this country who play consecrated drums.[21]

The African influence permeated the secular music that Santamaría played in Cuba. The lyrics of guaguancó and columbia are full of African words and allusions to Afro-Cuban belief systems. While the verse may be in Spanish, the choral response is often in an African language. These inserted African passages are a typical feature of much Afro-Cuban songs, whether rumba or *el son*, and contribute a quixotic aspect to their meaning.

The dances themselves have their own form of inserted African passages. In yambú, for example, the woman may momentarily move using the symbolic gestures of various deities, she will raise her arms and then rub her body in the manner of the oricha, Ochun. Or she may make the percussive arm dives of Chango that resemble lightning bolts. In guaguancó and columbia, a rumba dancer may momentarily move in ways that are markedly atypical of rumba dancing. He or she might fall to the ground in the ritual salutation known as moriforiborele, or suddenly kiss a person on both cheeks.[22]

Cuba has had a long tradition of Black string players. Violinist Claudio Brindis de Sala (1800–1872), is regarded as one of the greatest Cuban musicians. In contrast to the United States, Black string players performed in the same groups as whites, and they constituted a substantial part of Cuban symphony orchestras.[23] The violin was considered a respectable instrument that could provide an Afro-Cuban youth with a profession. This was certainly among the reasons Santamaría's mother encouraged him to take violin lessons.

My mother wanted me to play the violin. She would send me to the academy when I was a kid to learn the violin, but I was really intrigued by percussion. I would go to school to learn but the problems which filled my mind were those of percussion, and that's the way it was. I kept on, kept on, kept on, and I dedicated myself to percussion formally.[24]

Although he is best known for playing the conga drums, Santamaría started his career playing the bongos. In fact, the conga did not enter commercial music groups in Cuba until the 1940s.

[I used to borrow the bongos from] a little white guy called Siboney. . . . And then he would want it and send someone after me to get it and they wouldn't find me and those typical kid things. And then there was a man from Spain, named Jaime. He made the best bongos in Cuba. and I gave him three pesos and he gave me a pair of bongos, all golden, all rounded and not joined together like they make them [in the United States]. I have a pair now that I got from Germany and they make them that way too: completely complete. I'd sit there for two or three hours with the bongos.[25]

You had to be a good bongo player to play. So I began to feel good with the bongos, and I got so excited about them. They spoke to me so strongly that nobody had to teach me or anything. There was a guy named Chicho [Clemente Piquero] who played with Beny Moré for a while. Chicho was a phenomenon. I never saw anyone play like him, not from Africa, not from Cuba, not from anywhere. I would go with Chicho and play the tumbadora [the lowest-pitched conga drum] and also repique [usually called the quinto, the highest-pitched conga drum]. I would play everything because I learned a lot from Chicho—because he could play everything.[26]

Santamaría, like other drummers of his generation, learned music in the streets by observing different drummers. When he started playing professionally, he learned on the job. His approach to the instrument was utilitarian, not theoretical.

When I play I don't know how I do it, or what I do. People have asked me how many times I hit with the right, the left. I just play.[27] In Cuba it's different than here. When I came to the United States I was surprised because I saw a lot of things that I never saw in my life, like people going to school to learn to dance. In Cuba, that sort of thing was something natural. If you got it, you got it. That's the way it was. If you really were able to do it, they recognized you and gave you an opportunity; if not, they stopped you right from the start. Anywhere there was anything concerned with music, to play drums, I was there. Then I became a professional, just like that.[28]

Santamaría's first big job in the music world came in 1937, when he joined the Septeto Boloña, a *son* group, and stayed for two years. The group's leader and namesake, Alfredo Boloña (1890–1964), was one of the first *son* musicians in Havana.

El son is the guitar-based music of Cuba from Oriente Province. A *son* group's ingredients are a bongo player, a few singers who also play maracas, claves and guitar, a bassist and a tres player. The tres is a guitar with three sets of doubled strings with a distinctly smoky sound. However, *el son* may also be performed by a solo singer accompanying himself on a tres or guitar. The essential qualities of *el son* are a relaxed tempo and mood, reminiscent of its rural origins.[29]

El son came to Havana as a result of a 1909 edict by President José Miguel Gómez transferring soldiers away from their place of origin. He was fearful of army uprisings, and this was his solution. "The soldiers from Oriente brought *el son* to the capital, while the inhabitants of Havana introduced the guaguancó to Oriente."[30] The first group in Havana was the Trio Oriental, which was made up of musicians in the standing army from Santiago, Cuba: tres player Sergio Danger, guitarist Emiliano Didull and bongo player Mariano. *El son* quickly found a home among prostitutes and gamblers and was condemned by all but the poorest Cubans for its lowly origins. The authorities hated it because soneros had a habit of incorporating insults into their lyrics and their public performances often erupted into riots. Soneros also took aim at corrupt politicians. As its popularity grew, soneros were careful to avoid the sort of lyrics that got them into trouble, and by 1924 *el son* was welcomed by upper-class Cubans, although it was occasionally subject to official censure. Like upper-class white American devotees of New Orleans jazz, rich Cubans enjoyed being able to temporarily imagine themselves as members of a racy demimonde.

And like New Orleans musicians, the musicians who played *el son* were able to become professional musicians.

During the daytime Santamaría played on radio station *Mil Diez*, the Socialist Party station. The Socialist Party had bought the station "by virtue of public subscription" (*mediante suscripción popular*) in the late 1930s or early 1940s.[31] Santamaría played bongos with the Orquesta Cubaney on a lunch-hour broadcast. The Orquesta Cubaney "played everything," Santamaría remembered. "They had Bebo Valdés, great musicians, the greatest musicians in Cuba." He also performed and recorded at the radio station with Celia Cruz and Puerto Rican singer Pedro Flores. In the late 1940s, Salvador Diaz Versón, the president of the Anti-Communist League, threatened a boycott of any company that advertised on the station. After the advertising revenue dried up, musicians such as bandleader and flutist Antonio Arcaño continued to perform live at the station without pay for an entire year to keep the station afloat, but it soon closed for good.[32]

During the 1940s, Santamaría performed with the house band at the Tropicana, led by singer Alfredo León. According to Santamaría, the musicians "were very well known and professional musicians: Joseito Muños, Humberto Bello, the pianist Tibio Contrera, another phenomenal pianist in Cuba, Cristóbal Duran, who played the tres and also an incredible composer, Miguelito Pallazo who played the trumpet, Daniel Bonbolé who sang."

Santamaría remembers the Tropicana as "one of the most beautiful cabarets ever seen in the world. American tourists and millionaire Cubans would arrive at the Tropicana in a yacht. They'd all get really drunk and break everything in sight. Then they'd spend a bunch of money. They'd spend 30,000, 40,000 pesos on roulette."[33]

In Graham Greene's 1958 novel *Our Man in Havana*, Jim Wormold, the vacuum salesman who makes up espionage stories in order to run up his expense account as a British spy, takes his daughter out to the Tropicana for her seventeenth birthday: Greene describes the interior of the famous nightspot as a series of roulette rooms through which visitors passed on the way to the 1,000-seat Paradise Under the Stars:

Stage and dance-floor were open to the sky. Chorus-girls paraded twenty feet up among the great palm trees, while pink and mauve searchlights swept the floor. A man in bright blue evening clothes sang in Anglo-American about Paree. Then the piano was wheeled away into the undergrowth, and the dancers stepped down like awkward birds from among the branches.[34]

The main attraction at the Tropicana was the showgirls, who before the revolution were invariably mulatto.[35] They dressed in the sequined and revealing costumes found throughout the world—"their nakedness covered only by three sequined triangles in front, and a thong and a single poof of ostrich feathers in back."[36] The Tropicana showgirls also wore clothing inspired by Santería such as full-length white dresses and head beads. The evening's entertainment often included real or imitation Afro-Cuban music and dancing, including bembe, rumba and comparsa (the infamous conga line).[37]

In addition to playing with Alfredo León, Santamaría occasionally appeared in the floor show. One of these was *Congo Pantera*, a legendary show with a musical ensemble made up of some of the best rumberos in Havana plus a ballerina from the Ballet Russe.[38] The show's central number was a piece entitled *Parampampín* composed by conguero and columbia dancer Chano Pozo, who gained fame as a member of the Dizzy Gillespie orchestra. Santamaría cites him as an important figure in the popularization of the conga drum:

You can't say how great the Gillespie/Pozo relationship was. The importance is blurred a little. You accept the conga now, but it was only bongos and timbales at one time. . . . Chono gave ideas to Diz—the bottom. Al McKibbon was the bass player then. He told me that they couldn't get it together at first. It is important that the bass player and the conga player coordinate. Chano couldn't speak English, that made it even harder because McKibbon couldn't speak Spanish. It was a musical thing that brought it off.[39]

Congo Pantera was put together by choreographer David Lechin and Gilberto Valdés, one of the few white musicians in pre-World War II Havana with a profound knowledge of Afro-Cuban music. Valdés was born in Bemba, which Santamaría describes as being 99.5% Black.[40] He used his knowledge of Afro-Cuban music and applied it to his symphonic work. He figured as an important informant to Fernando Ortiz, the author of several groundbreaking treatises on Afro-Cuban music. He was also a flutist; he recorded an album with Dizzy Gillespie called *Dizzy Gillespie and His Latin-American Rhythm* that contains the first recording of Gillespie's famous composition *Con Alma*.[41]

Santamaría and Valdés collaborated several times in the United States. The percussionist was in a charanga group led by Valdés when it appeared in New York, the first time such an ensemble was heard there. Valdés's flute can be heard on Santamaría's *Drums and Chants* recording made in 1955. In the United States, Valdés was Katherine Dunham's musical director. "Nobody could put the drum and the big band together like Gilberto. He went back to Cuba after Castro took over and they gave him a big house. I don't know what happened, but he came back here again and died in Miami."[42] Santamaría remembers Valdés with fondness. He was very happy when arranger Marty Sheller sent him a photo of the flutist.

Santamaría told me that he saw a program on television in July 1999 that featured a show at the Tropicana "with all the saints, Yemayá, Obatala, all of them, all of them, all of them. A beautiful, beautiful, beautiful show, very similar to the David Lechin show."[43]

Silvestre Méndez was also in *Conga Pantera*. He was Pozo's brother-in-law. As a young man, Méndez moved to Mexico. According to Santamaría, "He went to Mexico when they grabbed him with a packet of grass in Havana. So for 40 pesos he was let go. He was able to leave without papers or anything!"[44]

Santamaría met fellow bongo and conga player Armando Peraza during the time Santamaría was already recognized as one of the top percussionists in music and Peraza's career was just starting. Peraza, who gained fame in this country as a member of Santana's group, became one of Santamaría's best friends and close musical associate. "I heard him play and I knew he was a brother without having spoken to him or anything. And there was a very friendly feeling between us. We became friends, like brothers. He'd come over to my house and have lunch with me."[45] They were a percussion team for many years, first in Mexico and then in the United States. Peraza was born May 31, 1924, in Havana, Cuba, in a neighborhood called Lawton Batista, a few miles from the center of Havana. Orphaned before he was a teenager, Peraza sold vegetables from a heavy cart to make a living before he started in music. He began his professional career when he joined Conjunto Cubavana in 1944, one of the most popular groups in Cuba at that time. Patato Valdez and Peraza teamed together in the group, with Valdez playing conga and Peraza bongos. During that time he also recorded with Pérez Prado. Around 1947, he joined El Bolero, replacing Mariano, one of Cuba's bongo-playing masters and a founding member of the Trio Oriental. Then he replaced Mongo Santamaría in Los Dandys. Cuban musicians used to ask him, " 'Who's better? You or Mongo?' I'd say, 'Mongo is better than me.' "[46]

Peraza followed Santamaría to Mexico and then the two congueros wound up in New York City. In 1953, Peraza joined up with George Shearing and stayed in the British pianist's group for a decade. He and Santamaría were bandmates in Cal Tjader's group when Tjader recorded Santamaría's classic, *Afro-Blue*. He has recorded as a sideman with Santamaría on several albums. Armando Peraza found fame and fortune as a member of Carlos Santana's group. He can be heard on many of Santana's recordings, such as *Caravanserai, Illuminations, Welcome, Love Devotion Surrender, Inner Secrets, Oneness: Silver Dreams–Golden Reality*, and *Marathon*.

What was it like being a musician in Cuba? Mongo Santamaría hated the racism and lack of respect:

The San Souci [nightclub] then was like Texas—discrimination. The band had to go around to the kitchen to get in. We couldn't mix with the customers. And you never saw one black face in the audience. Most of the audience every night was American.

When I was young I would never see those things. I would play with the kids and we never cared, light or dark. When I got into the profession, I played with everybody and they had to use me because I was good.[47] Those old people in that movie *Buena Vista Social Club*, they're 90 years old. They never had any chances. They grew old, and nothing happened. One time in Cuba there was a problem with color. I used to play good, yeah. But one band, they were white people. They used to call me to make a recording. But they didn't want me in the band on stage. That's what it what like in those days. You worked good and everything, but you never had any chances. In the nightclubs and everything there was too much discrimination. That happened in many places. But today you have white and Black together. That band, Irakere [a Cuban jazz band of the 1980s that included Arturo Sandoval and Paquito D'Rivera], was whites and Blacks together, and they didn't have any problem. That problem was eliminated. A lot of things in Cuba the American people don't know about. But I was born over there. And I saw many, many things, in the nightclubs, many things that were happening over there. I can say because I went through the thing.[48]

Armando Peraza enjoyed being a musician, despite the discrimination: "For you to make a living in Cuba playing bongos you have to do something right. A lot of people play this. And I was recognized for what I was doing; I made a living playing bongos. We started at 9 P.M. and played until four, five o'clock in the morning. I played every night, every night. I made about $10 a night. That was good money. The groups I played in played for tourists and Cubans, Black and white. We played the same music for all audiences. People danced; they didn't sit down and listen."[49]

Not all musicians shared Peraza's enthusiasm. Trumpeter Felix Chapotín, who remained in Cuba after the revolution, remembers playing on an empty stomach: "Sometimes things would get all blurry, or I'd even black out. And if that happened to me, with a steady job, you can imagine what other musicians went through."[50] And then there was corruption, which strangled Cuba's cultural life in myriad ways. Cuban musicians avoided the Cuban record companies like Panart by producing their own tapes and sending them to the United States.[51] Unless the musical group was well known, the musicians were under the mercy of a system in which payment was given in full only when the house was full.[52]

Santamaría and his friends often worked in first-class nightclubs. But most Black musicians performed in the second- and third-class nightclubs along the beachfront areas of Marianao or the docks in Habana Vieja. These clubs survived through the mid-1960s, when Castro outlawed all privately owned businesses.[53] Afro-Cuban musicians who played *el son* also found employment in the *academias de baile*, dancehalls where men paid to dance with white women and light-skinned mulattas who were usually not averse to accepting money for sex. The white patrons of these "dance academies" were among the first outside the Afro-Cuban communities to hear *el son*. Shortly after the music had become established in the *academias de baile*, the owners of Cuba's breweries got the idea to hire *son* musicians to perform in the gardens surrounding their factories. At first, the main patrons at beer garden dance events were Afro-Cuban, but after about 1927, white workers came as well.[54]

The Afro-Cuban middle class gave very little support to *el son*. Middle-class Afro-Cubans had their own exclusive social organizations (*sociedades de color*). They forbade the use of "street drums" such as the bongos and tumbadora, and established a Comisión de Orden that monitored the sort of dancing that was allowed.[55] The music they preferred was *vieja trova*—popular songs patterned after Italian arias.

While in Cuba, Santamaría delivered the mail.[56] The position of mailman was one of the few government jobs that Afro-Cubans could get, and for that reason Santamaría held onto it despite his many gigs in the music world. When the dancer Pablito Duarte asked him to come with him to Mexico, Santamaría was reluctant to give up the job.

But I spoke with an old mailman, Don Alberto Gomez, who was called "Don" because he was a Cuban patriot who had fought in the Cuban Independence War. He was a very wise man. He told me, "In 20 years you will be as you see me now: carrying mail, no money, and without hope of reaching retirement. So if you are good in music, get out now and leave Cuba." So I went to the guy who was making all the arrangements and said: "Tell Pablito that I'm coming to Mexico." So I made my decision, and then I told Peraza that I was going to Mexico and when I got there I would send for him, and that's how it was.[57]

By the time Mongo Santamaría moved to Mexico in the late 1940s with the dancer Pablito Duarte and his wife, Lilón, Mexico had become a second home for Cuban musicians. Santamaría was very fond of Mexico and its people. "It had a totally different lifestyle. I was very happy in Mexico, very happy."[58] "When I got to Mexico it was so different. I felt free. It was 'Señor Santamaría.' Nobody had ever called me that. I was somebody."[59] Although he loved the country, Santamaría knew that some day he would have to leave for professional and financial reasons. "In Mexico they charge you in Mexican pesos. It was very heavy in your pockets. But when you exchanged it, it was worth nothing. And I had family, I had my mother in Cuba I was sending money to."[60]

Mexicans had fallen in love with Cuban music ever since the Cuban danzón, the formal dance played by groups known as charangas or danzóneras, was introduced in Mexico at the tail end of the nineteenth century.[61] The timbale player, Babuco, whose real name was Tiburcio Hernández, was the first Cuban musician to have a career in Mexico. He had come to Mexico while traveling with a circus band and soon started his own danzónera. His band played in Veracruz, the danzón capital of Mexico, at the opening of the dancehall El Salón Mexico. Aaron Copland immortalized El Salón Mexico in his composition of the same name. As is typical in Mexican groups, Babuco had a *secre*, literally a "secretary," who acted as a band boy carting instruments and also as an extra percussionist. Babuco's *secre* was the timbalero Acerina, who was soon to become the most famous Cuban bandleader in Mexico.[62]

In the 1920s *el son* arrived in Mexico. The first *son* group in Mexico was called Son Cuba de Marianao. In the 1940s, the most famous Cuban sonero of all time, Beny Moré, came to Mexico toward the beginning of his career as a substitute member for an ailing Miguel Matamoros in the famous Trio Matamoros.[63] He later performed with Cuban pianist and father of the big band mambo, Dámaso Pérez Prado, who came to Mexico around the same time as Santamaría.

Percussionists such as Santamaría, Peraza and Méndez arrived in Mexico after a network of nightclubs and dancehalls dedicated to Cuban music was already in place. In addition to bringing rumba to Mexico, they spread their religion, which attracted many Mexican followers. Santamaría and other Cuban drummers performed with Moré and Pérez Prado. They also worked with Mexican groups. Santamaría played with the Mexican *son* group, Son Clave de Oro. Silvestre Méndez found a niche in Mexican films influenced by the floor shows at the Tropicana. Exotic dancers such as Tongolele, Kalantán, Ébano and La Diosa Rubia performed a variety of styles, but their forte was Afro-Cuban production numbers choreographed by Cuban dancers such as Pablito Duarte.

Although Santamaría thought that Duarte was a fantastic dancer and his wife was very beautiful, the job with Duarte was full of tensions. Initially they didn't want to hire Santamaría.

Originally Pablito wanted Chicho, but he was too busy, so Chicho suggested me. They didn't want to accept me at first because I was a muchachito del barrio [little ghetto boy]. They didn't trust me. But when I played the bongo, Pablito didn't want Chicho anymore, just me.[64]

The troupe of dancers and musicians, which also included Armando Peraza, made its way to New York for six months in 1948. Here, Peraza and Duarte had a huge fight. After that, Peraza and Santamaría went back to Mexico, and found themselves unable to work due to visa restrictions. So they returned to Cuba. While in Cuba they found out from the newspapers that Duarte had killed his wife and then himself.

5

Santo and Santamaría in the United States

Nobody was playing batá. Nobody was playing chekere. And today you see the Puerto Ricans, the Dominicans and everybody play everything because the people became fanatics, and started to learn one way or another. And they play![1]

When Mongo Santamaría came back to New York with the citizenship papers he needed in tow he found his way into a select coterie of Cubans, Puerto Rican New Yorkers, and African Americans devoted to Afro-Cuban religion.[2] It was a small group consisting of just about 25 people.[3] Santamaría, like others already in this circle, became a guiding light in the expansion of Afro-Cuban culture in the United States. At that time, there were three principal figures in Afro-Cuban culture in New York: Machito, Chano Pozo and Pancho Mora.

Pancho Mora was the first babalawo (literally, "father of the mysteries") in the United States.[4] The babalawo is the high priest in Santería and a master of divination. Mora, whose religious name was Oba Ifa Morote, was born in Cuba in 1903. He came to the United States in 1946 and started his religious house (ile) in New York shortly thereafter. Santamaría attended celebrations at Pancho Mora's house when he was living in an apartment on Seventh Avenue and 112th Street.

Machito (Francisco Grillo) grew up in Jesús María, the same barrio that Mongo Santamaría and Silvestre Méndez lived in. Before he left Cuba in 1937, Machito had been a respected member of Cuba's musical community, in which he had been a sonero and maraca player in a few sextetos (Sexteto Occidente, Sexteto Nacional, Sexteto Agabama and Sexteto Universe).[5] In 1940, the big band group Machito and the Afro-Cubans was born. Led by vocalist Machito and the Cuban multi-instrumentalist Mario Bauzá, the big band developed a sound in which Afro-Cuban rhythms met big band instrumentation halfway. Out of this orchestra came much of the Afro-Cuban music that flourished in the next decade. When Cuban musicians came to New York, their first stop was Machito and the Afro-Cubans. Nearly all of them knew Machito in Cuba. They ended up playing in Machito's group or in the orchestra of Tito Puente, the Puerto Rican New Yorker who began his career as a teenaged trap-set drummer in Machito and the Afro-Cubans.

Jazz musicians came to Machito and Mario Bauzá to find Cuban musicians. It was through Mario Bauzá that Dizzy Gillespie discovered Chano Pozo (Luciano Pozo y González). Pozo, born in Cuba in 1915, was a singer, dancer and conguero. He began to attract attention as a member of the Conjunto Azul, which also included his half-brother, trumpeter Felix Chapotín, and as the well-dressed figure leading the comparsa group Los Dandys through the streets of Havana. In 1946, he came to the United States and became the protégé of Machito and singer Miguelito Valdés. He recorded with both of them, as well as with Arsenio Rodríguez, who was visiting New York at the time.

But it was with Dizzy Gillespie that Pozo gained immortality. He was the first conguero to play with a jazz group in which he put his knowledge of Afro-Cuban folklore to good use. He performed with a flashy showmanship that he had perfected in Cuban cabarets. Jazz musicians tended to confuse his performances with the real thing and believed that Afro-Cubans considered his use of religious music sacrilegious. But Cubans were used to these staged versions of Afro-Cuban music. When Pozo was murdered in a Harlem bar, jazz musicians spread a rumor that he was killed for performing sacred Afro-Cuban music in public. In fact, Pozo was angry at a drug dealer by the name of "Cabito" Muñoz for having sold him 25 cigarettes of oregano instead of marijuana.[6] A fight started, and Muñoz shot Pozo. Because he was a decorated World War II veteran, Muñoz received a light sentence of five years.

Soon after Santamaría moved to New York, Francisco Aguabella and Julito Collazo arrived with the Katherine Dunham dance troupe. Then, with a ticket paid for by Santamaría and Peraza, Carlos "Patato" Valdez came to New York. By the mid-1950s there were enough Cuban musicians with a background in folklore and popular music to capitalize on Chano Pozo's success. They performed the music a bit more authentically than Pozo. For one, Pozo played the music as a soloist when an ensemble was actually needed.

In 1955, Mongo Santamaría recorded the first U.S. album of Afro-Cuban music. *Chango*, rereleased several years later with the better known title *Drums and Chants*, remains one of the most influential Afro-Cuban recordings here in the United States. It included an assortment of secular and religious rhythms that, at the time of the recording, were nearly completely unfamiliar to jazz and Latin music fans in the United States. Santamaría chose musicians with a knowledge of Afro-Cuban rhythms that, in some cases, exceeded his own. Although Santamaría was intimately familiar with current rhythms, he needed specialists like Julito Collazo and Silvestre Méndez to help him with more obscure rhythms. Other musicians on the recording were Patato Valdez, singer Marcelino Guerra and Antar Dali. An unexpected addition to the session was the flute of Gilberto Valdés. "He wasn't supposed to play!" Santamaría told me. Gilberto Valdés, who Santamaría remembers with much fondness, was apparently so moved by the drums that he *had* to play. Valdés's flute adds an exquisite and unexpected coloration to the drums-and-voices instrumentation.

The drawback of this recording is that on several of the selections conga drums were used in lieu of the idiomatically correct instruments. One can't fault the musicians, since at the time these instruments were not to be found outside Cuba. Although it has been supplanted by many recordings that are entirely authentic, it still retains its strength decades later.

The story of the making of the recording gives a picture of the chaotic lives these musicians lived. And, as is often the case in Latin music and jazz, the musicians were in conflict over who deserved recognition for their creations. In this instance, Silvestre Méndez believes that Santamaría took credit for an album that was intended to be his.

Méndez was on the road with singer María Antonieta Pons when he came to New York City. He remembers that Antar Dali introduced him to George Goldner of Tico Records as a possible successor in the field of Cuban folkloric to his late brother-in-law, Chano Pozo. Goldner expressed interest in producing a recording, and Antar Dali then assembled the musicians. They rehearsed under Méndez's supervision at Machito's home. "I did everything, I composed it, I directed it," Méndez remembered. The rehearsal was conducted in a party-like atmosphere, with the musicians sharing a bottle of Matusalén. According to Méndez, Mongo Santamaría subsequently persuaded Goldner that it would be better to put the record out under Santamaría's name. If there was a demand for a follow-up recording, he would be available, while Méndez would be back in Mexico.[7]

Mongo Santamaría disagrees with Méndez's account. He told me that he, not Méndez, had forged the connections with the recording company. It was not Silvestre Méndez's record, but his alone. Here is Santamaría's recollection of the classic recording:

[Méndez] saw me at the Palladium and we went to hang out. And I said, let's do this record. And he said, OK, it's a great idea. And then we got together with Antar

Dali. I think Dali was from Matanzas. He was very crazy. He died, and they found him full of coke. Doing coke at a performance and, anyway, he burned himself. And also, oh, I can't remember his name, a guy who died, a Jew who had a Puerto Rican wife—a real nut. He came to a rumba at my house and we agreed that he should play also. Anyway, he sang backup and so did Marcelino Guerra's wife. Everyone in the group was Cuban except for Willie Bobo.

We had done eight numbers with Silvestre Méndez and they had sold so much that a guy [from the record company] said he wanted four more tunes. Silvestre had already gone back to Mexico, so we got Julito Collazo and we did four more."[8]

I was paid $80 for that recording and each sideman was paid $40, without any kind of contract. *Chango* is the best album recorded in the United States within that genre, much better than *Yambú* and other albums which I recorded later for Fantasy Records.[9]

DRUMS AND CHANTS:
COMMENTS ON A FEW SELECTIONS

I reviewed a few of Santamaría's records with John Amira, a New York City *batalero* and coauthor with Steven Cornelius of *The Music of Santería: Traditional Rhythms of the Batá Drums*.[10]

Margarito

This song is a guaguancó composed by Silvestre Méndez named for the child of a washerwoman whose services Méndez relied on at his home in Mexico City. The lyrics run as follows: "Margarito, you like guaguancó, but I like bembe." *Margarito* is a guaguancó. After *Margarito* came out, Tito Puente took a fancy to it. He arranged it for his big band and recorded it with the singer, Santitos Colón.

Druma Kuyi

This song by Silvestre Méndez is identified as batá on the liner notes. No batá drums were used at the session (there may have been none available at the time). The drums are playing an approximation of iyesa, a category of Afro-Cuban rhythms that has been incorporated into Santería ritual in the United States.[11] The infectious lyric ends the verse with *Pa'que lo baila niche nganga* ("in order that the black priest can dance"). Although the piece has a certain value as a typical cabaret version of Afro-Cuban song, Amira considers it to be a watered-down iyesa or makuta.

The performance begins with a long trilled shiver *brrrrrrr*, which possibly has a semantic value, since extraordinary vocal quality plays an important role in Afro-Cuban religious music. The lead singer in an Afro-Cuban religious group sings in a pointedly altered manner, usually with a raspy timbre. By contrast, the choral response is delivered in a normal, no-frills voice. The lead singer's object is to come up with an other-worldly timbre in order to meet the spirits halfway and entreat them to descend to earth.

Morforiborere

Julito Collazo is the lead singer here. Collazo has a voice that is well liked and readily identifiable to aficionados of Afro-Cuban music. According to Amira, the album *Chango* was initially a 10-inch recording featuring Silvestre Méndez. When the recording went to the standard 12-inch LP, three additional compositions with Julito Collazo were added.

Morforiborere (also spelled *Morforiborele*) is the traditional greeting given to Santeros. This performance is batá playing adapted to conga drums, with the low tone of the iya (the largest batá drum) replicated by the conga drum playing a heavy bass tone. Amira assumes that Patato is the one imitating iya, since he heard Patato doing this in a performance. There are two songs played here. In Santería it is standard practice to lead from one song to another, a process called *secuencia* ("sequence"). A better translation would be "medley." The first two lines of the first set of lyrics are identical to lyrics given by John Mason in his groundbreaking anthology of Lucumí lyrics, *Orin Orisa: Songs for Selected Heads: E lu be sango* ("You pierce and slice, Shango"), *E lu be amalá* ("You pierce and slice yam porridge").[12] Amalá is also cornmeal, and in Cuba it is common to hear the Yoruba word used for cornmeal, just as the Yoruba word *quim-bombó* is a commonly used synonym for "okra."

Congo Mania

This is a traditional comparsa song. Comparsa is the carnival music of Cuba from which the conga rhythm derives. The arrangement, a medley of several songs, features two unnamed trumpeters. The recording attempts to create the feeling of a comparsa group, which consists of approximately 30 members, including dancers, horn players and singers.[13]

Caumbia

Although this composition is credited to Patato Valdez, Amira believes it to be a traditional song. In part it is about a conflict between the Con-golese people and the Carabalí people from the Calabar region of western Africa. Amira believes that Collazo is the lead singer and Patato, the quinto soloist. The refrain, divided between chorus and lead singer, goes: *"Cara-balí y Congo Reales estaban en porfía"* ("Carabalí and Congo Reales were in a conflict").[14]

Abakuá (Ecu Sagare)

Silvestre Méndez is the lead singer. Carabalís in Cuba formed secret fraternal organizations, which Amira likens to the Masons. Their members were called Abakuá or ñañigos, the latter term originally being pejorative. In addition to Black Abakuás, there were groups of white Abakuás in Cuba from the early years of the twentieth century. Amira believes that there are Abakuá societies in Miami, but he knows of none in New York. Unlike other African survivals that have been dispersed throughout the Caribbean and South America, the Abakuá seems to have taken root only in Cuba and nowhere else.

Yroco

Silvestre Méndez is the lead singer in a performance that reminds one that Méndez, like his brother-in-law Chano Pozo, was a cabaret performer whose forte was participating in staged versions of Afro-Cuban folklore. Although the performance tends to be overly theatrical, the songs in the *secuencia* are entirely traditional. Iroco (the more common spelling) is the ceiba tree. It is considered a sacred bush, and the orisha of the Immaculate Conception.[15] The piece begins with the drums playing a fast set of triplets while singers chant, "Iróco, Iróco, Iróco." Afterward, we hear Méndez reciting a series of African words connected with Abakuá, and then a few words connected with obi, the Yoruba divination practiced using four pieces of coconut. Méndez announces the last word, *"alafia"* ("health") with a hearty laugh. The rhythm shifts into a 2/4 pattern consisting of even eighth notes with an anapestic stress: 2 *and* 1, 2 *and* 1, 2 *and* 1, Amira considers it another watered-down version of iyesa. Méndez sings *Ir-o-co, Ir-o-co, Ir-o-co*, following the pattern stroke-for-stroke. After Méndez completes his verse, it is repeated by a chorus and then by flutist Gilberto Valdés's improvisation. After a few verses, the rhythm switches back to the triplet pattern heard in the beginning with a new song. Both songs in the sequence resemble lyrics found in John Mason's anthology. The first is: *Ko, Ko, Ko, Iroko moye sa* ("To capture, capture, capture, Iroko knows the value of time"). The second is: *Soro ka o ku yeye* ("Talk reaped long life for mother").[16]

Ochun

Silvestre Méndez is the lead singer. Ochun is the daughter of Yemaya. She is "the source of life for the world . . . the patroness of Cuba. . . . Osun represents females in power, controlling not only law and economics but the ability to market their own natural resources . . . She is the champion of women and the protectress of mothers."[17] Amira recognizes the second song as a common praise chant to Ochun.

Oromiso

The lead singer is Julito Collazo. This song is another chant for Ochun; it is an iyesa rhythm. According to Amira, the high and middle drums are correct, but the low drum is playing the wrong pattern.

Bembe Kinigua

The piece begins in 6/8 at a medium tempo in the rhythm known as batirí, for which Antar Dali is regarded as the creator. Amira told me that batirí is used as a warm-up in Cuban folkloric dance classes. *Bembe Kinigua* ends in a terrifically fast rumba columbia.

Consejo al Vive Bien

This song "exemplifies a genre frequently encountered in the rumba—the ethic of the unreconstructed macho hustler, the *vive bien*, 'livin' good' off his woman's favors.' "[18] Amira guesses that Patato's song ("Advice to the playboy") refers back to the song *El Vive Bien* sung by Roberto Maza on the album *Guaguancó Afro-Cuban con Roberto Maza y el Coro Folklórico de Alberto Zayas* that came out on the Cuban label Panart (LP 2055) several years before the *Chango/Drums and Chants* session took place.[19] Amira is pretty sure Julito Collazo is the lead singer and Patato Valdez is the fantastic quinto soloist. As with most of the selections on the recording, it is a medley. The second song has the line *"Kuenda Maria."* Amira informed me that *Kuenda* is Congolese for "go" or "walk," a command directed to the nganga spirits to come. *Maria* is a reference to Maria de la O, an early nineteenth-century musician whose life history has been the subject of many fictionalized accounts.[20] Like Cecilia Valdés, another nineteenth-century woman, Maria de la O has been immortalized by Cuban writers and musicians as the archetypical beautiful mulata.[21]

In 1956, Mongo Santamaría organized an homage to the saints at the Palladium. It was the first performance of this kind. "The Americans came and filled the Palladium. Fantastic! We did all the things: guaguancó, columbia, santo." At the time Santamaría, Collazo, Aguabella, Valdez, Carlos Vidal, Peraza, Cándido Camero, and a few other Cubans were the only musicians here who could put on such a performance. Things have changed greatly since then. "There are many people here now who can do these things. Puntilla (Orlando Ríos) is here, and there are a lot of people in

Central Park [rumberos]. There are a lot of Cuban Santeros."[22] Puntilla, a Cuban who came to the United States during the *Mariel* boat lift in 1980, has a reputation for being the best Afro-Cuban specialist in the country; Santamaría respects him, but considers him overpraised. "No, he plays very well. [But] it's like they said about Chano Pozo, that he was better than anyone in Cuba. Ha, ha!"[23]

In 1957, Tito Puente recorded an album of Afro-Cuban music, called *Top Percussion*, with Santamaría, Francisco Aguabella, Julito Collazo, Enrique Martí, Marcelino Guerra, El Viejo Macucho and Merceditas Valdés and Willie Bobo. Because of Puente's fame, this recording had perhaps the greatest impact on Americans than any other recording in the Afro-Cuban genre. The emphasis is on Lucumí praise chants. Julito Collazo is the lead singer on *Eleguara, Bragada, Oguere Madeo* and *Obaricoso*. Aguabella sings lead on *Obatala Yeza* and *Alaumba Chemaché*. There is a comparsa featuring Santamaría on quinto and a selection called *Ti Mon Bo* in which Santamaría, Puente and Bobo (on bongos) take turns soloing with a bass accompaniment. The title has an Afro-Cuban ring to it, but it is simply the first syllable of the names of the three percussionists. Santamaría's solo begins with *tumbao*, the standard conga riff in popular music, and he returns to *tumbao* after each foray into a soloistic improvisation. He also shifts into a 6/8 mode, demonstrating the metrical elasticity of much Afro-Cuban influenced music. According to Victor Rendón, who transcribed the entire solo, "This recording was the first instrumental hit in the New York City Latino radio circuit in the early 1960s."[24]

Yambú came out in 1958 on the Fantasy record label. The recording is similar to *Drums and Chants*, but Santamaría considers that a better recording. Francisco Aguabella is the singer featured on most, if not all, of the Afro-Cuban religious music, taking up the role that Julito Collazo and Silvestre Méndez were responsible for on *Drums and Chants*. As on Puente's *Top Percussion* and *Drums and Chants*, Santamaría is featured on a comparsa. Here, the name of the selection is *Conga Pa Gozar* ("Conga to Enjoy"). Unlike the comparsa on *Drums and Chants*, this one is pure percussion—no instruments or vocals.

The liner notes by Dick Hadlock are filled with misconceptions. He describes the song *Mi guaguancó* as "a rumba, named after a district of Cuba, that reflects more of the Spanish influence, though it is basically in 2/4 time." He speaks about the conga drum as follows: "Its potential as a means of telegraphy between restive villages (it can be heard for miles) once caused the Cuban government to outlaw the big drum." Hadlock offers only faint and damning praise for *Yambú*: "As one learns to accept the drum as an instrument of melody, capable of syncopated, contrapuntal, expressive music, Afro-Cuban music becomes a stimulating and rewarding experience." Disregarding the success of Santamaría's earlier recording and Puente's *Top Percussion*, he sticks to a misbegotten thesis that Americans have difficulty listening to real Afro-Cuban music because they are locked into "a rigid concept of melody which we regard as omnipotent."[25]

YAMBÚ: COMMENTS ON A FEW SELECTIONS

Longoito

Mercedes Hernández is the lead singer on this praise chant to Oya. The lyrics, which are in John Mason's collection of chants, are as follows: *Oya mi lo ya, Oya mi la ya, Oy mi lo ya Oga bembé* "The tearer shakes, twists, tears [2×], The tearer who shakes, twists and tears is a Stout Superior").[26] Oya, the daughter of Yemaya, is called the tearer because of her fierceness. In some legends she is married to Ogun, who first discovers her when she is in the form of a buffalo. She changes into a beautiful woman and makes Ogun's first wife furious. Oya turns back into a buffalo and gores her to death. Oya eventually tires of Ogun and leaves him for Shango, with whom she is closely affiliated in rituals.[27]

Bricamo

Yambú contains one of the few, if not the only, recorded examples of *bricamo*. Bricamo is the name of a society akin to Abakuá, but one in which women as well as men may be members. It originated in the Niger Delta. In Cuba, bricamo was practiced only in Matanzas Province, where Aguabella grew up. Bricamo is also defined as "a ritual dance where participants cleanse themselves and their surroundings with branches of green leaves."[28] As performed on *Yambú, Bricamo* is pure dance music, little more than a rhythmic pattern in triple meter with countless repetitions whose function is to provide a background for dance steps. Lest the reader think that such a description smacks of ethnocentric narrow-mindedness, I wish to point out that Fernando Ortiz, the dean of Afro-Cuban scholars, noted a similar quality for an Abakuá dance in which a seven-piece percussion group "constantly plays the same basic rhythm in order that the *diablito* dances."[29]

Yambú

The title track is a typical yambú, the slow couple dance that antedates the guaguancó. Its words closely resemble the *Yambú Matancero* published in Cuba's National Folkloric Company's brochure:[30] One line of the lyric goes: *yambú de tiempo España*—"yambú from the Spanish era." Spanish-era rumbas were no longer commonly practiced even during Santamaría's youth. The yambú is performed on packing crates, recalling the days when rumberos made their money as dock workers, and rumba was regularly heard on the docks. The lyric *el yambú no se vacuna* reminds the couple dancing that, although they may be flirtatious, they aren't supposed to engage in *vacunao*, the rooster-and-hen game of sexual conquest that characterizes guaguancó. Bassist Al McKibbon is a member of the chorus on *Yambú*. Santamaría wanted him to participate on the recording simply because the two had become friends. Because McKibbon didn't speak Spanish, he had to learn the words phonetically.

Timbales y Bongo

This track features Santamaría on bongos, the instrument on which he gained his reputation when he was still living on his native isle. Here he plays the instrument with sticks, giving it an entirely different sound quality.[31] The timbales player is Willie Bobo, Santamaría's protégé in the world of Afro-Cuban music. Francisco Aguabella serves as a bridge between the two soloing percussionists by playing a trio of conga drums. In this era, playing three congas at a time was a novelty; a decade earlier the practice was unknown.

In 1960, Santamaría and Willie Bobo went to Havana to record two albums for Fantasy Records, one devoted to popular music, and the other to folkloric music. The latter album, entitled *Bembé*, was probably the first recording of batá by a commercial recording company based in the United States. The batá drummers are identified by first name only. Most likely, they are Jesús Pérez, Mario "Papo" Angarica and Alfredo "Coyude" Vidaux (identified, respectively, as Jesús, Papo and Alfredo).[32] *Bembé* was Santamaría's last full-length recording of Afro-Cuban folklore, and it is his most authentic. Religious songs are sung by Merceditas Valdés and Mongo Santamaría's cousin, Luis. Merceditas Valdés was a well-respected singer for Santería rituals. She gained fame in the 1940s from her appearances on Radio Cadena Suaritos's weekly programs of Afro-Cuban songs. In the early 1950s, she recorded Lucumí praise chants on the Cuban Panart label.[33] Luis Santamaría has a voice as harsh as Valdés's is sweet, but it is powerful and very effective. Santamaría visited his cousin Luis the last time he returned to Cuba. "Luis is blind but still practices Santería. He's blind but still does all the things pertaining to it perfectly well."[34] *Bembé* also has several rumbas, presumably with Mongo Santamaría playing quinto. Carlos Embale, who sang on the Panart recording *El Vive Bien*, and Finco sing two guaguancós written by Francisco Aguabella: *Agua Limpia* and *Complicaciónes*. Merceditas Valdés sings the rumba columbia *Ochun Mene*, whose lyrics comment on how beautifully Ochun and Shango dance. Other singers are Macucho and Mario Arenas.

I discussed with Santamaría several controversial issues within the Santería community. For many members of the religion, the saints were nothing but a ruse to enable adherents to worship African gods in peace. Since people can now practice the religion in the open, it is no longer necessary to refer to the orishas by their Catholic names. In Cuba, people now refer to the religion as *la regla de ocha*—"the order of the orishas." Santamaría told me that this is, in fact, the correct name, but he has no problem with the name Santería. Santamaría has the tendency to refer to the saint name first, and then add the Yoruba name. In effect, he hyphenates the names.

There is a racial divide in the practice of Santería—at least in the United States. Some African Americans have started a movement to eliminate much of the Spanish vocabulary of the religion. They favor the African practices over the Cuban ones. There is disenchantment among this group over the large number of white devotees who have flocked to the religion in recent years. According to Santamaría, the santeros in Miami are nearly all light-skinned Cubans. "It's the evolution of life. And nobody's going to stop that."[35]

6

Santamaría Away from the Source

Many immigrants leave their country behind with few regrets. No matter how much potential they have, political forces and prejudices have kept them from attaining success. Santamaría certainly felt this way. He could be the best percussionist in Havana, but he'd never make more than 10 pesos a night. It wasn't bad for a *muchachito del barrio*, but Santamaría wanted more.

When he became a fixture in the New York City Latin music scene, he realized that he would always identify himself with Cuba. When I spoke with him in 1999, almost sixty years after he left Cuba for good, he still was referring to the island as "my country." Most of the music he performed in the early 1950s was Cuban, or based on Cuban models. Bandleaders would fly to Cuba to shop in music stores for the arrangements of the leading Cuban bands. But, as Santamaría quickly found out, the majority of the musicians in New York knew about Cuban music only from records. He found that they often lacked a certain tone quality or rhythmic conception that kept them from playing or arranging in a true Cuban style. In the United States, he realized that musicians were unsure about clave, the rhythmic keystone of Cuban music. "In Cuba, we don't think about that. We know that we're in clave. Because we know that we have to be in clave to be a musician."[1]

Santamaría has adopted the role of guide-to-Cuban-music for several American musicians. Willie Bobo was Santamaría's most receptive student, and the one most able to take Cuban music and make it his own. When Santamaría recorded Cuban folkloric music, he brought along Willie Bobo, in part to give the Nuyorican musician a musical experience. Soon after he joined Tito Puente's band, he became Tito Puente's Cuban music guide.

When I was with the orchestra, I showed him a lot of things: Look at this, listen to this. Also with the cha cha chas—all those things from that era. I had a lot of records that came from Cuba that I showed him when he came to my house. I'd give them to him and he'd copy them and do the arrangements.[2]

When Puente expressed an interest in rumba and other percussion-based Cuban traditions, Santamaría was happy to steer his Cuban friends in Puente's direction. Santamaría sang his friends' songs to Puente, and then Puente arranged them for his big band. This is how Francisco Aguabella's guaguancós *Agua Limpia* and *Complicaciónes* entered Puente's repertoire. Another song Santamaría introduced was Silvestre Méndez's song, *Margarito*, which Santamaría had recorded on *Chango*. Puente's arrangement of *Margarito*, which came out a year later on the RCA Victor album *Carnival Cubano*, was the source of the first argument between the two musicians:

It was a great arrangement but I didn't think the clave was right. During the rehearsal we had an argument because while they were singing it wasn't right. I was following them, but I understood that it wasn't working. He got pissed off with me during the rehearsal and put the song away. But a few days later we sat down at the piano and I told him how I thought it should go. We fixed it and until today he plays the tune the way we arranged it that day.[3]

On the one hand, Santamaría must have been happy that his boss took an interest in guaguancó and, later, Afro-Cuban religious music. After all, Santamaría was an expert in this area of music, and Puente was willing (at least in the recording studio) to give Santamaría the spotlight. But he was deeply disturbed by musicians playing Afro-Cuban music who knew nothing about where the music came from. The music is inextricably linked to feelings generated by specific times and places that non-Cubans can't easily understand. He believes that it is impossible to capture the qualities of the music without those feelings:

You can't learn to play things like guaguancó here [in the United States]. You have to have been where it came from to know that you kill or get killed for women . . . and drums. You have to understand ñañigo, Abakuá. Cándido, Peraza, Patato, Francisco Aguabella. You can't listen to records and get those feelings.[4]

Santamaría resents the fact that Puente was given credit for his own musical accomplishments. Puente had much greater fame than Santamaría, so his recordings of songs that Santamaría taught him were much better

known than Santamaría's. What really irks Santamaría is that he has never
been credited for the song *El Cayuco*.

El Cayuco was stolen by Tito Puente from me. *El Cayuco* was mine! And when I
left his band and went to California with Cal Tjader, he put it under his name! . . .
The great one of the mambo wasn't Tito Puente; it was Pérez Prado. There's a
mistake here, a *wrongness*. . . . There are a lot of things that have been said that
are not true! The tunes that have been stolen, the names that have been removed.
Lots of music, lots of music. Like Marcelino Guerra's music. He was a great singer
and composer, and they took his name away. His songs were hits all over the
world.[5]

In 1957, Santamaría and Bobo left Puente and joined vibraphonist Cal
Tjader's Latin jazz group. The move introduced Santamaría to an entirely
different lifestyle. He and Bobo had to move to the West Coast, which was
Tjader's home base. His record company, Fantasy, was also on the West
Coast. Santamaría found himself enjoying playing outside the small Latin
areas of a few major cities:

It was too limited: you were playing in the "barrio" in Manhattan, but outside,
there was nothing happening. I went with Cal Tjader after Tito Puente and we
played for five thousand, ten thousand people, and I saw how the people were
crazy about the music. In order to sell records and achieve popularity and to get a
name, it was more convenient to play in that way than to play *típico*. If I had
wanted to play *típico*, I would have stayed in Cuba! I never got away from my
background, but to push the music, to accomplish something big, you have to be
in the majority. . . .
   Today it's about 32 years since Chano Pozo got killed. He was the most known
conga player in the world. You know why? Because he was playing with Dizzy
Gillespie. He was exposed to everybody. I used to play with Tito Puente at the
Palladium, and the people who knew me were the people in Manhattan—nobody
else! When I went with Cal Tjader, I played in the universities, concerts with Nat
King Cole, with Count Basie, playing everywhere. Six months later, the people knew
me better than in the seven years with Tito Puente.[6]

Tjader was completely different from Puente. While Puente performed
for dancers, Tjader played for listeners. While Puente performed almost
exclusively for urbanites, Tjader performed for a wide audience—in jazz
clubs, festivals and college campuses. Puente's audience was primarily
Latin, especially on the West Coast, while Tjader's was mixed. While
Puente featured himself, Tjader let everyone in his group shine—especially
the two-man rhythm section of Santamaría and Bobo. While Puente dom-
inated his group, Tjader let his sidemen contribute compositions and arrangements. Tjader recorded several of Santamaría's compositions.[7]
   In the summer of 1958, not too long after Santamaría joined Cal Tjader's

group, Fantasy Records began to develop Santamaría's career as a band-leader. Within a year and a half Santamaría put out four records. Santamaría's inclination was to return to Cuban roots and surround himself with Cuban musicians. Aguabella, Duran, Vidal, Bobo, and McKibbon appear on both *Yambú* and *Mongo*. *Yambú*, which I have described in depth elsewhere, was Cuban folkloric music. Unlike *Drums and Chants*, Santamaría's earlier recording of Afro-Cuban music, *Yambú* reached a large jazz audience simply because Fantasy was a well-established jazz label. *Mongo* was a foray into the sort of Latin jazz that Tjader had found success with: improvised jazz solos and prominent Afro-Cuban drumming. *Our Man in Havana* and *Bembe* were recorded in Havana, at the tail end of the Cuban Revolution. The original record label bears the inscription, "Recorded under the personal supervision of the Fidel Castro regime."[8] *Our Man in Havana* features cha cha cha songs in which Santamaría's conga drumming is relegated to the background, and includes Santamaría's popular tune *Vengan Pollos*.

Afro-Blue, Santamaría's most famous song, received its first recording on *Mongo*. It is difficult to imagine a more incongruous setting for the creation of *Afro-Blue*: backstage at the Los Angeles television studio of the *Dinah Shore Show*, where Tjader's band was waiting to perform. The following night the band played *Afro-Blue* for the first time. It has been recorded by a number of jazz musicians including John Coltrane, with whom it is so completely identified that many jazz fans think that he wrote the tune. *Afro-Blue* has provided Santamaría with a steady stream of income for forty years.

In 1961, charanga finally caught on. It was the pachanga, a fast dance invented by the Cuban Eduardo Davidson, that brought charangas into the Latin neighborhoods of American cities. The mambo big bands were too brass-heavy for the lithe music; it required the violins and flute instrumentation of the charanga. The music needed to be fast and with a light touch. The new craze created opportunities for two rising conguero stars, Ray Barretto and Mongo Santamaría, to start their own groups. Soon after Tjader left Fantasy for Verve, Santamaría took over the vibraphonist's spot on the Fantasy roster to form the group *La Sabrosa*. The group was made up of a few of Tjader's former sidemen plus musicians from Orquesta Ritmo Nuevo, a charanga group based in Chicago. Within a two-year period, La Sabrosa recorded five records. The group made a name for itself among jazz musicians. Although the group toured and recorded, the soloists became more immersed in jazz harmonies and blues licks—thankfully without losing their charanga roots. One of the violinists was José "Chombo" Silva, who doubled on his "real" instrument—the tenor sax. Silva played sax with a Lester Young/Al Cohn style, but his violin playing derived from both jazz and charanga.

Because of the music's style, Santamaría's playing is nowhere near as prominent as it is on Tjader's recordings. Santamaría recorded several of his own compositions, the most famous being the instrumental, *Para Ti.*

The group disbanded one evening in the Bronx, when a suitcase of Santamaría's containing cash and important documents was stolen. Santamaría suspected that one of the band members took it. After La Sabrosa broke up, Santamaría signed with Riverside Records, an East Coast-based record company devoted almost exclusively to jazz.[9] Santamaría formed a new group with horns instead of violins. The recordings that surfaced in the months after he formed this band indicate that Santamaría was determined to steer his band toward an American audience.

From the old group he kept Julito Collazo and Victor Venegas, the Mexican-American bassist for Orquesta Ritmo Nuevo. The rest of the group were Americans with a background in jazz. The lineup featured a trumpeter and two saxophonists who doubled on flute. Over the next few years, Santamaría siphoned musicians away from the Hugh Dickens band. The list of musicians includes Chick Corea, Bobby Capers, Rodgers Grant, Marty Sheller, Bobby Porcelli and Hubert Laws.

Hugh Dickens was a tenor saxophonist who had a big band, and then a jazz sextet, that played in the African American social scene in Harlem and the Bronx. Dickens and the other bandleaders on this circuit such as Joe Panama (real name, David Preudhomme) and Henry "Pucho" Brown played for fashion shows, cocktail sips and "chicken and booze" dances, in which audience members brought their own food and drink. The clientele expected to dance to a wider variety of music than their white counterparts, and were accustomed to the music being played authentically. As a result, "It was taken for granted that a musician working the 'chicken and booze' circuit would be able to play jazz, rhythm and blues, calypso, and Latin."[10] Trombone legend Barry Rogers was the musical director for Hugh Dickens, and he gave everyone a chance to be creative.

Pianist Chick Corea, who was to become one of the most respected pianists in jazz, was only 21 when he joined Santamaría's band. Saxophonist Pat Patrick, a long-time member of Sun Ra's Arkestra, was another charter member. The band went through a few personnel changes over the next few months. By the end of 1962, trumpeter Marty Sheller and Bobby Capers joined the band, and Corea was replaced by Rodgers Grant. Probably for the first time in his career as a bandleader, Santamaría was surrounded by musicians who didn't know much about Cuban music. Santamaría had to speak to them in English or have Victor Venegas translate for him.

In addition to appearances at top jazz spots like the Village Gate, Santamaría played at many of the same gigs as Dickens. Here he discovered that he had a real rapport with African American audiences. The music, composed by band members Marty Sheller, Pat Patrick, Rodgers Grant and

Hubert Laws, was often in a rhythmic hybrid of rhythm and blues and cha cha cha called cha cha funk that appealed to Black audiences. The song titles were usually in English.

While playing in a nearly empty Bronx club, Santamaría got lucky in a way that would never again be repeated. Chick Corea had given notice, and they needed a pianist to fill in for the weekend. Herbie Hancock was called in as a replacement. It was a somewhat unlikely choice, since Hancock had virtually no experience with Latin music. The band members taught him a little about playing montuno passages and told him to relax and enjoy the gig. Hancock recalls what happened the night that Santamaría discovered *Watermelon Man*, the only tune of Santamaría's to reach the top of the pop charts.

Anyway, the third day, that Sunday, we were actually playing in the Bronx, and I was living in the Bronx at the time. Donald Byrd, trumpet player, was my roommate, and he came. He was sort of like my older surrogate brother, more or less, you know. He came to this supper club to see me, working with Mongo, he wanted to see how I was doing. Anyway, during one of the intermissions, Donald had a conversation with Mongo something about, "What are the examples of the common thread between Afro-Cuban or Afro-Latin music and African-American jazz?" And Mongo said he hadn't really heard a thing that really links it together, he was still searching for it. And I wasn't paying that much attention to that conversation, it was a little too heavy for me at the time. But then all of a sudden Donald Byrd says, "Herbie, why don't you play *Watermelon Man* for Mongo?" And I'm thinking, "What does that have to do with the conversation that they're talking about?" I thought it was a little funky jazz tune.

So I started playing it, and then Mongo, he got up and he said, "Keep playing it!" And he went on the stage, and started playing his congas, and it fit like a glove fits on a hand, it just fit perfectly. And then one by one the other musicians got up and started playing the tune. The bass player looked at my left hand for the bass line, and he learned that, and he started playing it, and then the saxophone player, the trumpet player, pretty soon the whole band playing it. And also, little by little the audience was getting up from their tables, and they all got on the dance floor. Pretty soon the dance floor was filled with people, laughing and shrieking, and having a great time, and they were saying, "This is a hit! This is fantastic!" It was like a movie! So after that, Mongo said, "Can I record this?" I said, "By all means." And he recorded it, and it became a big hit. That's how it happened.[11]

During the recording of *Watermelon Man* for Battle Records, the producer, Pete Long, encouraged the band to make a three-minute rendition, suitable for radio play. The horn soloists avoided playing in a bebop vein. Santamaría and timbalero Francisco "Kako" Bastar played a cha cha beat and trap drummer Ray Lucas added a back-beat. In the next two months, everywhere people asked for two tunes: *Watermelon Man* and *Para Ti*. Sometimes the band played just these songs all night long.[12]

From July 1962 through February 1963, Santamaría recorded two records in addition to the album *Watermelon Man*. One of them featured a new Cuban sensation, La Lupe, whose complete name was Guadalupe Victoria Yoli. La Lupe had a tragic life that ended in sickness and neglect. But after she made this recording, she became a sensation. Her sexy and, at times, violent behavior set flames off on the bandstand. When she wasn't singing, she contributed orgasmic groans and encouragements to the soloists. Another recent Cuban arrival, trumpeter Chocolate Armenteros, was featured on La Lupe's record as well. In terms of Santamaría's career, the recording was a return to the source—back to Cuba with Cuban musicians.

Santamaría signed with Columbia and stayed with the company from 1964 until 1968. The label was determined to get Santamaría another hit record, as Marty Sheller recalls:

Everybody wanted to get another *Watermelon Man*, and Mongo was put in a very strange position. You have to recognize that *Watermelon Man* was not the typical thing that Mongo played. It was just because of the situation with Herbie Hancock and recording it and all. Everything else in Mongo's repertoire was not like *Watermelon Man*. But when he signed with Columbia naturally they wanted to take advantage of that. So they said to Mongo, we want you to do the *Watermelon Man* for the American people and then we want you to do a Latin album, a real typical Latin album for the Latin people, with different rhythms, with vocals, some instrumentals, that kind of thing. So Mongo did an album that I think was a real sleeper—people didn't realize how good it was. It was called *El Bravo*. [That album] included guajira, guaguancó, cha cha cha, mambo, merengue. Columbia wasn't into marketing in the Latin field very much so they didn't really promote it. But when it came time to record another album there were always suggestions from the company; they wanted to get another pop hit. . . . Because he wanted the record company behind him and didn't want to antagonize them, he felt that he had an obligation, plus they paid him some pretty good bread. Mongo wanted them to push the record, and they were not going to if they didn't feel like Mongo was giving them what they wanted . . .

Mongo's records always came out best when they would leave it completely up to him. . . . But a lot of times they wanted the input of helping choose material. . . . Mongo is a pro; the guys that he used in the band were very professional. So the album came out sounding professional but it wasn't a typical Mongo kind of album . . . but having the company suggest songs to do and those kinds of things, it put him in that bag where a pop artist is just as good as his last hit. . . .

What he did on the records was not indicative of what he was playing in the clubs. What he was playing in the clubs is what he was known for. When a new album came out, he would play some of the songs from it that were appropriate. But mostly he was playing jazz.[13]

In 1968, Santamaría signed with Atlantic Records, and for the next four years the label gave him a relatively free hand. One of the high points in these years was an appearance in front of a new audience: a concert at a large rock theater that included both the Grateful Dead and Jefferson Airplane. Santamaría struck up a musical friendship with rhythm-and-blues drum master Bernard "Pretty" Purdie. When I interviewed Santamaría, he related with pride how he played with Purdie on the 1968 hit single *Cloud Nine*.

IF THEY TELL YOU IT'S SALSA, IT'S A LIE: IT'S *SON!*

Many Cuban musicians who emigrate to the United States identify themselves as being part of an extended family of Cuban musicians on both sides of the sugar-cane curtain. They welcome touring Cuban musicians into their homes and help them out, since the Cuban emigrant population knows better than most about the abysmal state of the Cuban economy. When members of the Buena Vista Social Club came to New York, trombonist Juan Pablo Torres brought them to perform with him at a club near his home in Union City, New Jersey, and then took them to SOB's (Sounds of Brazil) in downtown Manhattan to sit in with Tito Puente. Mongo Santamaría is friendly with the members of Cuba's famous folkloric group Los Muñiquitos de Matanzas and socializes with them when they are in New York City. In general, Cuban emigrant musicians seem to be apolitical and don't hold a grudge against Cuban citizens. A few are quietly enthusiastic about the advances by Castro's government in the quality of life for Afro-Cubans and poor whites.

No matter how many years they have been in the United States, Cuban American musicians are proud of Cuban culture. However, many feel a close connection to Puerto Ricans as well as to Puerto Rican culture, and agree with an old Spanish expression: "Cuba and Puerto Rico are two wings of the same bird." Some Cuban musicians have found inspiration in both countries. For example, Cuban singer Justo Betancourt, who has lived in Puerto Rico for several years, leads a group called Borincuba. The name is an amalgam of Cuba and Boricua, the ancient name for Puerto Rico.

Santamaría sees danger in sublimating Cuban identity in the interests of a pan-Caribbean identity that Betancourt, Pupi Legarreta and many other Cuban American musicians revel in. He has taken on the role of defender of the dignity of Cuban culture.[14] One of his targets has been Fania Records, the Latin music label formed in 1964 by Johnny Pacheco and Gerry Masucci. Although Santamaría credits the success of Fania as "great for the musicians,"[15] he bemoans the fact that it has done a disservice to Cuban culture. Although the music recorded by Fania often included adaptations of songs taken from old Cuban records, the company wished to obscure its origins, partly because trade relations between Cuba and the United States were outlawed, but mostly as a marketing ploy.

When Fania artists recorded songs by Cuban composers, they made a policy of not listing their names. In the recording credits where the name of the composer usually goes were simply the initials D.R.—*Derechos Re-*

servados ("Reserved Rights"). The idea was that, due to the break in relations between the United States and Cuba, the composers would receive the money due them whenever relations between the two countries improved. As a result, the general public was not made aware of the tremendous amount of material by Cuban composers recorded by Fania artists. For example, on Ray Barretto's 1973 album, the wonderful *Indestructible*, half of the eight songs are listed as D.R.

The people at Fania knew enough about marketing music in the United States that they would need a label to describe their music and a publicity campaign to give it a legendary status. "Salsa" was the word that stuck. In Cuba, *salsa* (which means "sauce") was just one of the words musicians used to describe the flavor of their music. Other words were *saoco* and *sabor*. As a marketing device, "salsa" was a brilliant stroke—a new label for an old thing. It is *one* name for a cornucopia of Cuban styles—guaracha, guaguancó, santo, cha cha cha, son montuno, and so on—as well as the other Caribbean styles that the American bands covered like merengue and bomba. Advertising executives are not musicologists. One name, even if it is fabricated, is certainly more useful to them than 10 accurate names.

When the Cuban Revolution brought an end to the American tourist trade and prevented Cuban groups from touring the United States, Cuban music fans were offended that Cuban artists were not credited for their songs. And they were infuriated by the Fania-produced movie *Our Latin Thing (Nuestra Cosa)*, the first film made about Latinos and their music. To Cristobal Díaz Ayala, the author of a Spanish-language book about Cuban popular music, the movie suggested that salsa had come almost directly from Africa to lodge itself in New York, thus bypassing Cuba entirely![16]

Santamaría spoke about salsa and Fania's campaign of misinformation in a 1977 interview:

People don't recognize it as a Cuban thing that is very old. It did *not* filter through the Indies, then to Puerto Rico and Cuba, etc. Haven't you ever wondered about the differences between a calypso and a guaguancó? Between samba and guaguancó? It came directly from Africa to these places and stayed there. It did not travel on. There are different areas in Africa. Each area has its own music, religion and language. . . . It's still segmented according to the districts. Whichever type of slave was brought over, that's the kind of music that developed. In Cuba, they came from Yoruba, West Africa, the Congo and Guinea. So the music in Cuba is richer than in the other islands. You find the music in Havana different from the music in Oriente Province.[17]

Knowledgeable musicians are quick to acknowledge that salsa is just a branch of Latin music; the tree's roots are embedded deep in Cuban soil. But Santamaría goes a step further. Like the Cuban musicians who sang the words that form the title of this section, he questions whether salsa's newness is an inflated lie. Willie Colón is quick to respond to these criticisms of a musical style that he helped develop:

To say that salsa is *son* is just as ludicrous as saying salsa is bomba. It is an effort to reconcile all of the elements in our modern day lives, our roots, our stories. The seamless and truthful blend of three racial roots, African, European, and indigenous (Asian?). It carries pieces of our mythologies. It chronicles our slang and moves. It is also poetry, sometimes very political, sometimes social, sometimes gossip, and sometimes cheap shock. As such it will come to places where it can get saturated and corrupted. But because it is a popular music with an economic support base it is guaranteed to be able to change and live on.[18]

Colón sees nothing ambiguous about the term "salsa," among knowledgeable fans and musicians:

If you say Cuban *son*, people in Latin America will know what you're talking about. If you say salsa, they will also know that you're not talking about Cuban *son*. The Cuban contribution can never be denied but it is much more than a different flavor of Cuban music, much more. When Tito [Puente] says, salsa doesn't exist, I sometimes answer that I could say that Tito doesn't exist. That would also be incorrect. Salsa just is. Period. You know what they say: "50 million Frenchmen can't be wrong!"[19]

Colón delights in picking on his elders. He claims that he and his associates were criticized for juxtaposing song segments that contained rhythms from different countries—for example, "putting a bossa nova segment with a guaguancó, then a Puerto Rican aguinaldo." He suggests that their dislike of the term "salsa" is born of jealousy: "I understand that they resented the term 'salsa.' Maybe because they were not part of it."[20] It is not at all inconceivable that older musicians can become jealous of younger musicians who are stealing the spotlight away from them. But Tito Puente, Machito and Mongo Santamaría were not simply jealous. Instead, they were annoyed that young musicians—Colón in particular—were becoming stars despite their ignorance of the subtleties of Cuban music. In fact, Colón told the press that he enjoyed how his out-of-clave songs irritated the purists.

Colón skillfully frames his argument that salsa, a pan-Latin sensibility rather than a rhythm, is something new and original, and it is easy to be swayed. For Colón, the juxtaposition of, say, a guaguancó with bomba is what distinguishes salsa from Cuban music. The arguments about the existence of salsa go around in circles, with musicians blaming oranges for not tasting like apples. Beneath these arguments are a few difficult questions that I will leave the reader to ponder: How far can artists stray from the parameters of a style before it is ruined? How do you evaluate Cuban-influenced music that strays from Cuban prototypes?

In 1972, Santamaría hooked up with Fania Records, a move that was perplexing in view of his antipathy toward the main purveyor of salsa. However, the label had proved to be a ticket to international success for Latin artists. Over the next few years, Santamaría's relationship with Fania proved rewarding. Although his album *Amanecer* was the first Fania record to win a Grammy, Santamaría made no efforts to hide his criticism of the label. Santamaría recalled how upset his statements made Gerry Masucci, who called him into his office after reading Santamaría's statements in *Cashbox* and *Billboard*, two music trade magazines. Santamaría remarked in 1991: "The Fania All-Stars couldn't compete with any band from Cuba. Imitation will always be imitation."[21]

With *Ubane*, an album he recorded for Fania in 1976, Santamaría came close to proving himself wrong: salsa was not always an imitation of Cuban popular music. Unlike most of Santamaría's output, *Ubane* was recorded with a lead singer—Justo Betancourt, a Cuban immigrant a few decades younger than Santamaría—and a *coro* ("chorus"), the typical ingredients of both Cuban popular music and salsa. Therefore it is easier to compare it to Santamaría's *Our Man in Havana*, which similarly features a lead singer and *coro*. While that album is state-of-the-art Cuban popular music at the eve of the Cuban Revolution, *Ubane* is truly something different. It is a new sound. Dare I say its name: salsa!

In jazz, Santamaría found a home away from Cuban music. Santamaría could make a place in his jazz groups for the best jazz musicians he could find regardless of whether they knew Cuban music well or not. In the jazz world, he could function unencumbered by the ethnic tensions of the Latin world. And because he was an outsider, he probably felt himself to be uninvolved in the cultural tensions of the United States—in particular, the heated relations between blacks and whites. Over a period of three decades he surrounded himself with a vast number of international musicians to help define Latin jazz.

7

Jesús Caunedo

George Rivera and Charley Gerard

Many unsung heroes have participated in one way or another throughout
the history of what today some call Latin music. One who comes to mind
is the late, great pianist René Hernández, who was instrumental in developing the sound of the Machito Orchestra. We often neglect to pay homage
to these musical giants simply because they were never front and center.
However, we would be negligent if we were to disregard the contributions
made by these "invisible" men when writing about the history behind this
music. One such man is alto saxophonist Jesús Caunedo, who also plays
flute and clarinet. Jesús Caunedo has been an important ingredient in the
history of this music, having played with all of the most important musicians of his time (such as those of Machito and his Afro-Cubans, Tito
Puente, Tito Rodríguez, Apollo Sounds, and Bobby Valentín).

Caunedo was born in La Víbora, a barrio of Havana in 1934, and then
lived for many years in the barrio San Leopoldo. He started his musical
training in a school for orphans outside the capital. According to Caunedo,
you were considered an orphan at that time in Cuba if you did not have
a father, since few women worked. Around World War I there were many
children that were orphaned by the sailors that would come as a result of
the sugar trade. Caunedo's mother was alive but she did not earn any
money. Caunedo wasn't really interested in the school band, but the children in the band had certain privileges: They traveled to other towns for
parades and other events, and they were fed better than the other children.

Caunedo studied music at the orphanage with a teacher by the name of
Manuel García Gautier, who became a father-figure to Caunedo. During

vacations, Caunedo would stay in the school, and even though García Gautier was on vacation he would make the hour-and-a-half-trip to give extra lessons. García Gautier wanted Caunedo to be a classical musician, and he would have him practice on the clarinet seven to eight hours a day.

Despite, all the practicing, Caunedo was still able to hear the popular bands of the time. His favorites were Arcaño y sus Maravillas, a group that played live radio broadcasts, and Arsenio Rodríguez's conjunto. As a young man in Cuba and later in New York, Caunedo developed a friendship with Arsenio Rodríguez. He considers him to have been a natural musician with incredible abilities and an incredible ear. The blind tres player was able to recognize a person's voice even if he had not heard it in years. Caunedo also liked the Conjunto Casino, a trumpet band with creative arrangements that featured singer Roberto Faz. When Caunedo grew up, he became good friends with Faz. He considers him a tremendous gentleman, as well as a tremendous *sonero*.

When Caunedo started playing professionally, he was a part of a group that is considered to be the founding fathers of Cuban jazz. The drummer was Walfredo de los Reyes, a contemporary of Caunedo's who now lives on the West Coast. In Cuba, de los Reyes played with pianist Peruchín, who had a strong influence on New York salsa pianists. Papito Hernández, the bass player of Caunedo's group, later went on to play with Andy Williams.

Caunedo and his friends started a jazz club with the objective of bringing American jazz musicians over to Cuba with the money they made so that they could study with them. During that period, many American musicians traveled to the island. Caunedo and the other aspiring jazz musicians were able to bring them to a club for a small fee or sometimes for free. They would get musicians such as Philly Joe Jones, Stan Getz and Zoot Sims to come by. An excellent sax player by the name of Maurice Lewis helped Caunedo considerably. The visits proved to be a mutual exchange of musical traditions because the Americans were interested in Cuban rhythms.

The music of his country always grabbed Caunedo's attention. Not all Cuban musicians were as interested as he was in the island's sounds. He remembers that the show bands that played in the hotels in Cuba hardly played Cuban music. There were some secondary bands such as Riverside or Aragón at the Tropicana or Casino de la Playa at the Riviera, but the showcased bands were comprised of musicians that really didn't have an interest in Cuban music. When Miguelito Valdés would play the hotel circuit in Cuba, he would find himself in the company of Cuban musicians that didn't know much about Cuban music. Caunedo has known many musicians born and raised in Cuba that knew nothing about Cuban music and didn't understand the concept of clave. Caunedo believes that there was more of a preoccupation with Cuban music in New York than in Cuba.

Before coming to New York in the 1960s, Caunedo had already met most of the musicians that he would be playing with. He met Mario Bauzá when Bauzá presented the orphanage's band with certificates. However, Bauzá never heard Caunedo play. Tito Puente and Tito Rodríguez both saw Caunedo at the Hilton in Cuba where he was playing with Rafael Somavilla. He became friends with Chocolate Armenteros, who came to the United States shortly before him. When Caunedo decided to leave Cuba, he was unable to speak on the phone because all conversations were monitored, so he sent a personal message to Chocolate letting him know that he was coming to the United States. When Caunedo arrived, Chocolate introduced him to Machito, with whom Caunedo would record his first record, *The New Sound of Machito*.

Pianist and arranger René Hernández was working for Machito then. Caunedo considers this humble man to be one of the most important figures in Cuban music. Caunedo points out that the orchestra of Julio Cuevas was the first orchestra where the piano played the parts originally played by the tres, and where the horns played more than long notes. Cuevas's orchestra was the first where the sax guajeos were used, along with more intricate horn lines. These innovations were all because of René Hernández, Cuevas's arranger. Caunedo also credits Hernández with creating Machito's sound. Caunedo was honored to have René Hernández as his pianist when both of them had relocated to Puerto Rico. He was devastated when Hernández died on September 5, 1977.

Caunedo firmly believes that New York in the 1950s and 1960s was a locus of innovation in Latin music. An example he cites is the Machito Orchestra, in which jazz stars like Jerome Richardson, Cecil Payne and Doc Cheatham were playing rumba. It was a unique phenomenon that, in his opinion, couldn't happen anywhere else.

Caunedo willingly accepts the fact that ideas travel. He compares the internationalization of Cuban music to the spread of coffee cultivation from Arabia to the rest of the world. He take the Cuban bolero as an example: One cannot talk about the bolero without speaking about Agustín Lara or without mentioning the names of Rafael Hernández, Pedro Flores, Armando Manzanero, or Chico Novarro. Although they are not Cuban, their work is just as good as that of any Cuban artist. As for the danzón, the Mexicans have "Mexicanized" it so much so that it is played more today in Mexico than in Cuba. According to Caunedo, the same goes for what we refer to as "salsa" nowadays. Caunedo describes it as a manner of playing music with Cuban roots in an original and different way from what the Cubans have done, with a Puerto Rican flavor and originality. Caunedo believes that the contributions of Puerto Rican musicians have been great. For evidence of this one only needs to see that there are many Cuban singers today that are following the lead of Puerto Rican musicians. Besides appreciating the contributions made by Puerto Rican musicians, Caunedo readily declares his debt to Puerto Rican bandleaders like Tito Puente or Tito Rodríguez. They made it possible for the saxophonist to continue his career as a musician after he left Cuba.

Caunedo wishes that today's salsa musicians would pay more attention to the dancer. He notes that Puerto Ricans are currently enthused with the merengue. Why? First, one does not really need to know how to dance to enjoy it. Second, it is simple, rhythmically speaking. A merengue has that steady four-beat rhythm that even a deaf person can dance to. In Caunedo's opinion, the musicians that play salsa are so good and at times they get so carried away with their improvised breaks that in order to stay in step the dancer has to be exceptionally good.

8

Charanga and
Pupi Legarreta

Those of us who are jazz fanatics consider the use of a string section to be a commercial ploy to attract a larger audience with a patina of cloying, drippy sentiment. We cringe when we hear our favorite jazz artists playing with strings, because they are often a musical subtraction, not an addition. It therefore comes as a surprise when we hear music from other parts of the globe in which strings are successfully integrated into an exciting dance music. From Cuba comes such a music; it is called charanga. The ensemble that plays this body of music is itself called charanga, and it consists of a string section with at least a pair of violins and sometimes a cello, a solo flute and a rhythm section with timbales, bass, güiro, piano and congas. Although charanga is traditionally an instrumental form, it has evolved into a vocal music, typically featuring two male voices singing in unison.

Charanga is lithe and charming. It is exotic but reserved, rhythmically wild but holding back. Charanga is seductive in the same way that a half-exposed leg can be sexier than a bare one. According to Danilo Lozano, son of famed Cuban charanga flutist Rolando Lozano and himself a flutist and ethnomusicologist, charanga symbolizes the creole soul of Cuban culture:

The charanga represents a vehicle that has not only maintained the traditions of European and African conventions, but has incorporated folkloric Afro-Cuban rhythms. Through the creation of music and dance, a national style developed that merged these different styles and traditions to provide the foundation for a national Cuban expression.[1]

Charanga was a music with aspirations of respectability. As recently as the 1980s, charanga groups played arrangements of semiclassical favorites like *La Gioconda*. Charanga musicians were considered "educated" musicians. They took music lessons and attended music school where they were taught solfeggio and how to read music. As part of their training, they played in bands and chamber orchestras. Several prominent musicians such as Elizardo Aroche, Israel Cachao López and Orestes López played in symphonies in between charanga engagements. Before the Cuban Revolution, symphonic jobs were poorly paid, and most string players needed to play charanga to make a living.

The bongoseros, congueros and guitarists (I am including the tres in this category) in other popular Cuban idioms had a different musical and social background than charanga musicians. They learned their instruments on the street and didn't read music. In contrast to charanga musicians, they came from families that were participants in Santería and Palo Monte, and freely borrowed from the music surrounding these African-based religions. The lyrics they wrote were a melange of Spanish and African language idioms. While charanga musicians performed in "legitimate" establishments, *el son* was a music of the demimonde, associated with criminals and prostitutes[2] and with the debauched upper classes. Politicians and businessmen would hire *son* groups to play at *encerronas* ("lock-ins") for parties that lasted for several days, in which a small number of guests were invited to eat, drink and consort with prostitutes at a secluded location.[3] From the early years of the twentieth century, charanga appealed to both white and black middle classes, and it has been performed by Cubans of all skin colors. After 1940, mixed groups were common.[4] Since the 1920s, Blacks performing popular music were restricted to the percussion and bass, instruments they played in American-style dance bands like the one led by Moisés Simons at the Plaza hotel.[5] Not so in charanga, where Black violinists such as Enrique Jorrín played in integrated groups, and were universally recognized for their musical excellence.

Scholars agree that Spain and parts of West and Central Africa provided the most crucial musical influences in the development of Cuban popular and religious music. But in the case of charanga, the contributions of French and Haitian influences cannot be ignored. Charanga began its history in the early nineteenth century when Haitians, both African and French, escaped that island's revolution. They brought with them a love for the French contredanse, a multi-sectional dance form that evolved into the danzón, the quintessential charanga style. Both were performed by an ensemble called an orquesta típica, a group with brass, woodwinds and timpani that performed outdoors. When the upper classes decided to dance indoors, the instrumentation was radically altered. The new ensemble was called *charanga francesa*. Although the word *francesa* literally means "French," it was used in nineteenth-century Cuba more specifically as a

name for Haitian creoles.[6] In the charanga francesa, flutes and strings replaced the brass and woodwinds of the orquesta típica, and a small drum
kit called pailas (now called timbales) replaced the booming tympany.
While the orquesta típica was raucous in a New Orleans jazz fashion, the
charanga francesa produced a light and somewhat effete music.

The French influence extends to instrumentation as well. The flutist in
the charanga francesa plays a French baroque flute, a five-key wooden instrument with a meatier tone quality than the modern flute, and with an
entirely different fingering system. The instrumentation for the modern
charanga is based on the charanga francesa.

In the 1920s, el son began to be accepted by the middle classes, and
quickly began to eclipse the popularity enjoyed by charanga. Partly as a
means to compete for the public's attention, charanga musicians adopted
aspects of el son. The last part of the danzón became an improvised feature
for piano or flute. It was copied after the montuno, the improvised section
of el son. One reason el son was popular was that it was a vocal music,
so it was perhaps inevitable that Aniceto Díaz formulated the danzonete,
a danzón that featured vocals in several of its sections. In the 1930s, tres
player Arsenio Rodríguez added the cowbell to the son group, which, with
the addition of a piano and extra trumpets, had grown to become a son
conjunto. Soon after, timbaleros (timbale players) in charanga groups were
also playing cowbell.

By the late 1930s, charanga musicians had developed a sound with a
powerful rhythmic impetus that for the first time attracted lower-class Afro-
Cuban audiences. Pianists took to playing the typical lines of the tres, the
traditional guitar-like instrument featured in el son. Bassists patterned their
accompaniment after the tumbadora, the drum better known throughout
the world as the conga drum. Antonia Arcaño ("El Monarca"), the flutist
and leader of Arcaño y sus Maravillas, remarked that "blacks were the
connoisseurs of charanga and they were never wrong in the verdict. When
they proclaimed that someone was good, there was no doubt about it. They
told white people who stopped by to hear, 'Chico, go get Arcaño, who is
good.' And the whites would contract us."[7]

The tumbadora itself was introduced into the world of Cuban popular
dance music by Arsenio Rodríguez. Before then, the tumbadora was strictly
an instrument used in rumba or Santería festivals and ceremonies. Since
Arsenio's music was not considered high class, there were apparently few
social repercussions. But the musical changes were profound, and they
eventually spread to the world of charanga. Arcaño led the way, but at
first his group suffered the consequences of using an instrument connected
with Afro-Cuban street life. Arcaño y sus Maravillas was boycotted for
nearly a year, but after its fans got past the inclusion of the tumbadora,
they loved the tougher Afro-Cuban sound of the group.[8]

The two most influential members of Arcaño y sus Maravillas were the

López brothers, pianist/bassist/cellist Orestes and bassist Cachao, who together wrote thousands of danzónes for Arcaño. In 1938, they created the mambo. In its first incarnation, the mambo was a subsection of the montuno, with an unresolved harmonic pedal. The López brothers signaled the mambo to begin when the music needed a lift. The pianist played a syncopated line that was doubled by the strings in pizzicato mode. Danilo Lozano points out that "these elements, coupled with a change in dynamic intensity, created a tension with continuous repetitions. The effect was pronounced when it resolved to the tonic chord."[9]

A danzón with a mambo section was called a *danzón de ritmo nuevo*, a modern danzón, or a danzón-mambo. Eventually, the mambo section was taken out of the danzón form, especially by big bands in Mexico and the United States that took up mambo with a vengeance and made it a crazed, aggressive music. These bands performed whole compositions that began with the rhythmic interplay and instrumental counterpoint that had originally been meant to be a rousing climax that took place after a slow buildup of excitement and an almost imperceptible accelerando. In this respect, the big band mambo was out of step with Cuban musical tradition. As Cuban-American essayist Gustavo Pérez Firmat points out, "It has none of that 'parabolic enthusiasm' typical of other forms of Cuban music."

Arcaño's music was purely instrumental, and audiences began to miss hearing singers in the charanga format. And so when the cha cha cha was invented in the early 1950s by Cuban violinist Enrique Jorrín, it became an instant hit. Not only did it have lots of words, but it was easier to dance to than the mambo, and considerably less rhythmically volatile. Pérez Firmat believes that "in Cuba generally there was a fair amount of hostility toward the mambo, which was seen as a bastard child of the danzón."[10] There was also an element of patriotic hostility in their disavowal of the mambo because it had developed outside of Cuba by Dámaso Pérez Prado, who was considered somewhat of a renegade Cuban.

It wasn't simply that the new dance style had lyrics, but that the lyrics were gossipy in a way that Cubans adored:

Much of the interest of a cha cha cha resides in its picturesque, "newsy" subject matter—a curvy girl who wears falsies, a dentist who pulls teeth while drunk, a bald man who likes to go to the barbershop. Martians who dance. The cha cha cha imparts news or spreads gossip; it's a rumor mill, an example of what Cubans call *radio bemba* ["big-lipped radio"].[11]

Charanga continued to exist during the Cuban Revolution, but not without difficulties. Arcaño complained in an interview that took place in the 1970s that there were few good charanga players left. José Fajardo, a leading flutist and bandleader in Cuba, emigrated in the early 1960s along with several members of Arcaño's group. The band was returning from a Japanese tour. Instead of going back to Cuba, Fajardo and company sought asylum in the United States.[12]

> Afterwards, the bassist didn't want to play anymore and also left. The pianist became sick with thrombosis . . . I no longer had qualified personnel, because the group of charanga musicians was very small here. If one goes to make a recording it is necessary to use two violins from Barbarito Díaz, others from the ICRT . . . and so on.[13]

Despite the depletion of musicians, the musical landscape remained much the same, with nightclubs and private affairs providing a continuous source of work for musical groups of all kinds. When the North American market closed, charanga bands simply restructured their market, eventually finding new opportunities in France and Africa. Within a few years a new generation of charanga musicians were available. They had been thoroughly trained in the new and rigorous socialist regime, and were in some respects better equipped musicians than the generation they succeeded.

Directly after the revolution occurred, Pello el Afrocán came out with the mozambique, which was in essence a dancehall rendition of the comparsa, the Cuban Carnival street event. I am not aware why, or how, the music got its name. The mozambique derives from the name of an African nation; however, there are no Mozambican influences in the music. Cubans went for its intense Afro-Cuban street rhythms. The public's embrace of Pello el Afrocán's music along with the government's acceptance of Afro-Cuban culture inspired charanga musicians. Rumba clave replaced *son* clave as the new rhythmic guideline, forcing the development of new rhythmic patterns. Charanga groups such as Los Van Van (supplemented by a trombone section after the late 1970s) and La Orquesta Ritmo Oriental were in the forefront of a new style called songo. Their music was aggressive and rhythmically compelling. Rhythmic patterns that were standardized during the 1950s were tossed out by Cuban musicians.

CHARANGA IN THE UNITED STATES

The mambo and the cha cha cha were prominently featured in the burgeoning Cuban entertainment, broadcasting and recording media of the 1950s.[14] Not long after, the new rhythms caught on in the United States. Latin music audiences in this country were used to hearing Cuban music in big bands such as Machito and his Afro-Cubans, so the new dances were adapted for this instrumentation. In the process of being transmuted by Cuban expatriate bandleader and arranger Dámaso Pérez Prado in Mexico, the Latin big bands outside Cuba developed their own version of the mambo. Pérez Prado used a larger rhythm section than that found in a charanga band. It consisted of timbales, tumbadoras and bongos, the latter an instrument that until then had been exclusively associated with *el son*. Pérez Prado kept the basic idea of the charanga mambo, with its harmonic stasis, counterpoint and continuously repeated phrases. In big band mambo, a saxophone section and a trumpet section "perform passages in unison, and are in constant counterpoint."[15]

Along with the music, the dance steps of the mambo and the cha cha cha were changed when the dance styles stepped off the island. According to dance ethnologist Yvonne Daniel, mambo in Cuba "has a specific movement sequence; it has a different movement sequence in the United States and elsewhere, as it was popularized internationally."[16] The cha cha cha was misunderstood by non-Latino dancers. The motions of the dance are reflected by how it is meant to be counted: One, two, three, cha, cha, cha, two, three, etc. Note that the final "cha," in "cha, cha cha" lands on the first beat. In the United States, among non-Latino dancers, the cha cha is counted: one, two, cha; cha, cha, one, two, cha cha cha. Here the final "cha" lands on the fourth beat.

In the able hands of Pérez Prado, and Tito Puente, Machito and Tito Rodríguez, the mambo benefited from its translation into the big band. The cha cha cha was not quite as lucky. Because it was easier to dance to than other Caribbean and Brazilian rhythms, the cha cha became a favorite of society dance bands, who took away much of its charm. It was usually performed as an instrumental. Even if these dance bands were able to play in an authentic Cuban fashion, the instrumental cha cha cha, with its lack of rhythmic excitement, leaves something to be desired.

The charanga began its history in the United States as little more than a curiosity. Gilberto Valdés's charanga is considered the first charanga group in the United States. It made its U.S. debut at New York's Tropicana Club in 1950. Valdés is a fascinating musician whose music has sunk into obscurity. He was one of the few white musicians in Cuba in the 1940s through the postwar era with an extensive knowledge of traditional Afro-Cuban music, which he utilized in his symphonic writing. Mongo Santamaría was a member of the charanga. Since many musicians in the United States then were unfamiliar with charanga, Santamaría had to train the timbalero (Papi Pagani) to play the baqueteo pattern, the characteristic timbale part in danzón.[17]

It wasn't until 1959, when the pachanga, the fast Cuban dance attributed to Cuban bandleader Eduardo Davidson, made its way to the United States that charanga gained any lasting popularity. Charlie Palmieri's Charanga Duboney, with flutist Johnny Pacheco, quickly gained recognition. Mongo Santamaría's charanga group, which included Willie Bobo, flutist Rolando Lozano, violinist Pupi Legarreta and other fine musicians, gained an audience among jazz fans in addition to Latinos. Ray Barretto had a charanga as well, and made it onto the pop charts with *El Watusi*. Johnny Pacheco broke off from Palmieri and formed his own successful charanga. The Zervigón brothers (Eddy, Rudy and Kelvin) from Güines, Cuba, formed Orquesta Broadway in 1962, and José Fajardo established his own charanga.

Stateside charanga after the Cuban Revolution was patterned after Aragón, the Cuban group founded in 1939 in Cienfuegos by bassist Orestes Aragón. It has maintained the flavor of prerevolutionary Cuba. However, North Americans broke with Cuban orthodox practices by taking the flute and violin out of charanga and putting them in salsa bands in the company of trumpets, trombones and electric pianos. Art Webb, one of the best of the American Latin flutists, played in Ray Barretto's band alongside the trumpets. Típica '73 and later editions of this group freely combined aspects of charanga and conjunto in a jazz-influenced melange. Pupi Legarreta appeared as solo violinist with the Fania All-Stars, a conjunto-style group. Although North Americans might have been a touch more brazen than Cubans in the ad-hoc manner in which they assembled these hybrid ensembles, they were not the originators. For example, in 1958, trombonist Generoso Jiménez, his brother, saxophonist Enemelio Jiménez, and trumpeter Alejandro "El Negro" Vivar were members of Orquesta Sensación, a charanga.

Cuban immigrant musicians such as Fajardo, Zervigón and Legarreta preferred the five-key wooden flute that was part of the charanga tradition, while others preferred the modern metal flute. Unlike the five-key flute, the modern flute is capable of executing with ease the chromatic jazz lines that salsa arrangers write, and the newly invented contact microphones manufactured by Barcus-Berry and other companies made it feasible for the instrument to participate at nearly the same volume level as a brass instrument.

Charanga was inextricably connected in the minds of Latino audiences with the pachanga, a dance that proved too fast and difficult to maintain its popularity. When the pachanga craze ended around 1965, so went charanga, according to Latin music historian John Storm Roberts.[18] The Latino community in New York was changing, and its young people wanted a tougher, urban sound instead of a light-hearted Cuban one. But charanga never disappeared in New York. A portion of Latin music fans always seems to prefer charanga over salsa simply because they consider it more danceable.

At about the same time that charanga had lost its audience in New York, it was finding a new home in Miami's Cuban exile community. During the 1960s, danzónes and other nostalgic Cuban sounds were ubiquitous. In the 1970s, a new generation of Cuban musicians came into their own who were born in Cuba but raised in Miami. Charanga was the vehicle by which they started making their own music.

Two of the architects of the nascent Miami sound were Cuban immigrants Hansel Martínez and Raúl Alfonso who, after making a name for themselves in New York with Charanga '76, had moved to Miami to start their own group, Hansel y Raúl. Their charanga located its music in old Havana but its lyrics in Miami's Little Havana. They "discuss such subjects as alimony, the Florida lottery, intercultural romance, Japanese imports, drugs, women's lib, or the drudgery of getting up every morning to go to work—but always from a 'Cuban' point of view."[19] Hansel y Raúl delighted in talking about sex from a crude macho point of view. For example, *Esa mujer me gusta* ("I like that woman") is about a man seated on an airplane next to a woman with a big behind, and *El carro y la mujer* ("The car and the woman") is an extended metaphor about trading in the wife—the old car—for a younger woman—a new Japanese import. Their hit song *María Teresa y Danilo* is a spoof on Cuban American infidelities based on the television soap opera *Dallas*. Indeed, sex has always been a topic of charanga lyrics. For example, Enrique Jorrín's song *La Engañadora* is about a woman who fakes her sexy appearance by using falsies. Her ogling admirers ignore her completely when they find out that her appeal was just a padded illusion.[20] But in the lyrics of Hansel y Raúl sexual banter brings out "the clash of cultures" and "the dislocation of Cuban ways in a foreign culture."[21]

Hansel y Raúl was very lucky to have as its bassist Israel Cachao López, who left Cuba in 1962, lived in Spain for a year and a half, then permanently relocated to the United States. His brother Orestes López never left Cuba, preferring to remain there despite the hard years of the revolution when work became scarce and musicians were often cheated out of their pay.[22] In the 1990s, the Cuban American actor and bongosero Andy Garcia promoted Cachao's music and exhorted the Cuban American community to consider Cachao one of their cultural icons. Garcia directed and co-produced with Fausto Sánchez a feature-length documentary filmed in Miami about the legendary musician entitled *Cachao—Como Su Ritmo No Hay Dos* ("Like his rhythm, there is no one like him"). The documentary showed footage of a concert of Cachao's music, a rehearsal and a discussion with author Guillermo Cabrera Infante.

Through Andy Garcia's efforts, Cachao revived the charanga sound for a generation of Cuban Americans who were starting to forget their island's culture, and whose community was "thus far characterized by the predominance of culturally apathetic upper- and middle-class entrepreneurs and professionals."[23] Cuban Americans had reached a point in their exile when they, like other ethnic groups in the United States during the past two decades, were motivated by the search-for-your-roots fervor inspired by Alex Haley's book *Roots* and the television mini-series based on it. Helping them remember their roots and jump-starting the Cuban arts in Miami were the Marielitos, the wave of Cubans who left Cuba during the *Mariel* boat lift in April 1980. Among the Marielitos were a remarkable amount of talented writers (Reinaldo Arenas, Carlos Victoria and Andrés Reynaldo) artists (Juan Abréu, Victor Gomez and Gilberto Ruiz Valdez) and musicians

(Orlando "Puntilla" Rios, drummer Ignacio Berroa, and conguero Daniel Ponce).

There is a pivotal point in the documentary when Paquito D'Rivera, a member of Cachao's ensemble, is addressing the Cuban American audience. He tells them that when he first met Machito in New York, the bandleader told him that "the people who love Cuban music more than the Cubans are the Puerto Ricans." D'Rivera praises Puerto Rican musicians—in particular the members of Cachao's band, which included flutist Nestor Torres and tres player Nelson González—for keeping the flame of Cuban musical traditions alive in the United States. In effect, D'Rivera shames Cuban Americans for not appreciating their own traditions. Lending force to this sentiment is Cachao's postscript that appears after the final scene: "All I ask is for the youth to maintain the tradition."

The mambo big band, the Latin-jazz combo, and the salsa conjunto have been the sources of innovation for Latin music in the United States—not charanga. But in the last decade, charanga has been updated. Johnny Almendra and John Santos have embraced charanga in its new Cuban form, a reflection of the strong Afro-Cuban influence that marks postrevolutionary Cuban culture. In the 1980s and 1990s, the leaders of the new charanga groups had some difficulties finding string players who were interested in learning about charanga and developing their own styles within the tradition. But slowly they have developed a pool of violinists such as Sam Bardfeld and Venezuelan violinist Alí Bello who can contribute something valuable to the genre. Flutists such as Karen Joseph, who began her career as a member of Típica '76, are able to play fluently in the Cuban manner.

I suspect that the interest of the newest generation of charanga musicians in recent Cuban music is not shared by many older charanga musicians. One violinist I interviewed bemoaned that Aragón, whom he heard when the group finally was allowed to perform in the United States, had developed a sound in line with contemporary Cuban music: loud and overbearing.

FÉLIX "PUPI" LEGARRETA

Félix "Pupi" Legarreta is a violinist, flutist, singer, arranger, pianist and guitarist who has participated in several landmark periods of Latin music. He was born in Cienfuegos, the birthplace of a number of prominent charanga musicians such as Rolando Lozano, Rafael Lay and Efraín Loyola. He started his musical career in Cuba in the early 1950s when he was still a teenager, and played with some of the island's most famous musicians. He experienced the opulent nightclub scene that developed in Cuba after World War II and performed on live television. Like many other Cuban musicians before him he lived and worked in Mexico. Around the beginning of the Cuban Revolution he was given a ticket out of Cuba. In the

United States he joined the growing cadre of first-class Cuban immigrant musicians such as Patato Valdez, Mongo Santamaría and Rolando Lozano. After establishing himself as an artist, he began a long and successful association with Fania, the most important Latin music record company of the 1970s, recording under his own name and as a sideman with Johnny Pacheco and Larry Harlow.

Because he is primarily a violinist, Legarreta's career has followed the ups and downs of charanga in the United States. In this country, he began his musical life in Chicago, where he hooked up with the charanga group El Nuevo Ritmo. This group quickly made a name for itself and a classic recording, but was unable to keep up its own momentum. Legarreta and several other members of El Nuevo Ritmo joined forces with Mongo Santamaría when the conguero decided to become a full-time bandleader. After a year or so Santamaría decided to drop the charanga format and go for something more oriented to the American jazz and pop market, and Legarreta had to leave the group.

Legarreta's own debut was *Salsa Nova* (New Spice), which came out in 1962 on Tico Records. Fellow Cubans Patato Valdez on congas and vocalist Totico were featured on this recording. In the 1960s and 1970s, Legarreta recorded with Fania. Several records were collaborations with Johnny Pacheco, the artistic director of the famous label. One of the best is *Los Dos Mosqueteros*, which features the brilliant flutist Gonzalo Fernandez (mysteriously uncredited on the album notes). Legarreta played on Larry Harlow's *El Judío Maravilloso* and *El Albino Divino*. His work can also be found on Cachao's recording *Cachao y su Descarga, Dos* and with Orquesta Son Primero on the album *Charanga—Tradición Cubana en Nueva York*.

In February 1999, I traveled to North Philadelphia to interview Pupi Legarreta. He came in his car to pick me up at the train station. He apologized for being late, explaining that he had forgotten to fill the gas tank and had run out of gas, so he had had to fill a gallon milk container with gas and carry it back to his car. Legarreta is small, wiry and full of charm. He was an excellent interview subject. At the time of the interview, Pupi Legarreta was performing music as a sideline and studying electrical engineering.

Both Legarreta and his wife told me that Pupi was "into the music" and had no interest in Cuban politics. He admires the rigorous musical training that musicians receive in Cuba today, but seems to be dismayed by the grading system by which remuneration is determined. He told me how the government would not assign his friend and teacher Rafael Lay, leader of the famous charanga Aragón, into the top tier of musicians despite his reputation. Instead, Lay had to pass a program designed for training symphonic musicians, which he succeeded in doing. Legarreta has been back to Cuba just once—when he appeared with the Fania All-Stars at a Cuban festival in 1980. That was the last time he saw his mother. He continues to send her food and medicine through a Miami-based aid program.

The remainder of this chapter consists of extracts from my interview with Legarreta combined with material from David M. Carp's interview five years earlier. Carp has conducted hundreds of hours of interviews with members of the Latin music community.

Cienfuegos

I was born in Cienfuegos, Cuba, 1940. Cienfuegos is a big city. I'm from La Calle Cristina, very close to the ocean. My father was a barber. That's my first profession, barber. And at the barbershop with my father I used to practice the violin! (laughs) Almost all day! In Cuba you gotta study all day, believe me, to make it in music. In Cienfuegos, believe it or not, from that city we had great people there, like [sculptor] Arquímedes Pous. Everybody creates in there, it's like an island and you got the spirit from God. René Hernández is originally from Cienfuegos. And Brindis de Sala, too, the best violin player Cuba ever had. Classical violinist, he died in Argentina. He's the only violin player [who] ever opened this particular spot in the hand (points to web between fingers) to do the octaves and the tenths and things that they used to do. With the doctor, they cut open this particular spot.

I used to listen all the time when Orquesta Aragón had a radio program in Cienfuegos. And the other band was in there, too, Loyola. I used to listen to all the musicians from charanga style at that time. [Efraín] Loyola was the first flute player Orquesta Aragón had before Rolando Lozano. He formed his own charanga when Aragón got Rolando Lozano to play with the band [in 1950].

Studying the Violin

When I was about 10 years old I started to study the violin with Rafael Lay, the director of Orquesta Aragón in Cienfuegos. Lay was a—besides a strict [teacher] he was a very good friend of mine. He used to be a dental mechanic, that's how you call it? And he used to be close to me, you know, any help he asked me I give it to him, anything. He always treated me like family, you know, he was [an] incredible person about that. Very even, you know, he wasn't such a proud person, very human being, you know. And he treated me as family, he always clap, everything I do something he say "Go, man, very good!" And he was strict about the sight-reading (laughs), yes! The intonation I study, in Cienfuegos we got the strings, we study in someplace. But the brass, we used to study in a different place. I study the intonation with somebody there by the name of Peña, tenor player, in a different place, where they got like the brass and different things. I used to study in the daytime with Lay. At night I used to go with Peña in another place to study the intonation and things like that.

Rafael Lay, he did a type of small classical orchestra, like they call it *orquesta de camera*. Like—it was about six, seven violins. We got no cellos in Cienfuegos, we got the bass and we got some lady singing. And then sometimes we travelled to different cities to play with whatever we got. We used to play *Jalousie*, we used to play a couple of those semiclassical popular pieces in that band, I remember.

When I was studying with him I got the book, I opened the book, he marked me which one I have to study. I come back next week—"OK, you've got this one. OK, see you later, man, OK." When he comes back I open my book—OK, he opens the page, he knows which one he asked me to give at the lesson and he knows. If I don't do it right he says, "Man, you wanna do the other one? You don't got this one! You can start a little bit the other one but you gotta give me this one when you come back, man. (taps pencil) And let's go to the solfeo now, open the page, where are you now? OK, there, OK, let's see, man" (taps pencil in rhythm). Hits that with the pencil and he's giving me the rhythm (continues tapping), I'm singing and he's checking me out. And when you've got a teacher like that—I'm free, I used to pay nothing, you know. And that's the problem, how do you say, the pride of this teacher.

I remember when Lay used to call these girls over there and these people studying the classical over there in the school where we were. He used to say "Listen, I'm gonna give you [an] idea on why we don't practice so much of the classical." He said, "You see these people? You put that music away and these people, they cannot play no more" (sings Beethoven's *Für Elise* very mechanically). And besides that you cannot make even one dollar with that classical music. So we say, "OK, let's study the reading (claps hands) and go to the street with the band." We gotta study the books, how to move with the instrument, the bowing. But about the classical, the only thing we've got is that *orquesta de camera* that we've got in the school, you know.

Rafael Lay, he was a good violin player when he became famous with the Aragón Orchestra, about those years we mentioned, about 1955–1957. After he became famous for popular violin playing in Cuba he went to the school to get his degree. Because now with this system in Cuba if you don't got your degree you're not gonna get first payment check. You know what I'm saying? They've got different scales, like third and second and first. If you're not a good concert violin player, even if you're playing popular music you're not gonna get a first-class payment, you're gonna get a second- or third-class payment. So when I went back to Cuba with the Fania All-Stars in 1981, he told me: "Hey, Pupi, I went back to study and I graduated with the Concerto in D of Tchaikovsky." His son can play more than him. 'Cause these kids, you know, they're been studying with the Russians in there.

The problem with Lay was that Orquesta Aragón became popular and he left Cienfuegos. And for me [it] was impossible to continue studying with him. He used to teach at the Bellas Artes music school in Cienfuegos. So when Orquesta Aragón became popular he left Cienfuegos, so there was no violin teacher in the school. The only person I could go to was Santa Torres, his teacher. And she wasn't the teacher of this school; she was retired already. She used to listen only to classical music. She lived very close to where I used to live, she lived about one block from me. So I said the best idea, the best way I can follow the study of the violin is with this lady. She was his teacher and mine—as a matter of fact she was the owner of the house where I used to live in Cienfuegos.

Solfeggio

You had to do that in Cuba, yeah, you had to study the piano and the solfeo about two years. We studied *Solfeo de los Solfeos* and Hilarion Eslava. For the singing, Hilarion Eslava. The *Solfeo de los Solfeo*, that's the one we do, how do you say, with syllables. For the intonation we used Hilarion Eslava. *Solfeo de los Solfeos* had a lot of examples from different pieces—classical music from different big composers. And Eslava did his system different: he'd do different modulations and melodies.

Making a Living as a Musician

At the time even Lay was playing with Aragón he gotta work as a dental mechanic to make a living. And believe me, many days he came to me and said "Pupi, I need help." And that's nothing, you know, because we were musicians but especially him, he was [an] incredible musician at that time. But he wasn't making it with the music exactly. Aragón was the best band we got in Cienfuegos besides Argudín [?], alto sax from there, very good musician. And they weren't making it with the music—not even Lay, who was the best, you know? He's not even used to go to Havana [to] record or he was just conducting Aragón, writing a little bit for the group, getting some danzónes to put it together in the band and waiting for the break they got when they became popular, like around 1955.

In Cuba after four or five years of lessons and if you have a good ear, you've got to go to the street to make a living at music. I *was fast*: After two or three years I was playing professionally. About a year after [starting to study with Santa Torres] I went to Havana to play with Fajardo and Arcaño. From there I went to Sensación.

I played a lot of private places that they used to have in Cuba for the high-class people: Casino de Portillo, Centro Gallego. They've got these places where they make beer—Tropical, La Polad, those clubs. Whew! Thousands of people go to these places. Even now. The stadium where they play baseball they put the musicians in the middle there. All of Havana goes to those places.

We used to make about $10 to $15. Around 1959, the most I made was about $20. That was a lot. I was with Sensación, the best group at that time. Fajardo, Sensación and Aragón: the biggest charangas and most popular. When these groups played, you'd see people there, no doubt about it. That was good money. No problem. It's nothing now, but at the time it was money. I'd play three or four nights like that, make $100 a week at music—that was big money. Things there were cheap. You could eat with one dollar, good. In 1960, $20 was a lot of money.

The Musicians' Union

I was in the Musicians' Union in Cienfuegos and Havana. You gotta belong there, yeah. The violin player made more than the conga player. Like the flute player and the violin player and the piano player and the bass: they're making, you know, like $25, $30, you know, when the other ones, they're making $20, you know. That's true, yeah, OK. You know, a violin player is a person, the way they used to call that, that used to study the music. And the flute players and the piano players. Hey, this timbale and this conga player and this güiro from Cuba, at that time they don't know no music like now. [Today in Cuba] these conga players and these güiros and these drummers, they sight-read perfect. At that time this rhythm section, they don't read no music. You know how many times we had to rehearse a tune, wait till these people learn how to play that tune with all the breaks we use in those Cuban charanga tunes? Couple of days, we gotta come back to those re-hearsals to (laughs), to put this tune together. It's not one rehearsal like in here, sometimes we go to the studio with some music, probably the music that he would write (laughs) and we gotta fix it or "Let's go the way it is." Because no, in there they check the music or whoever checks the music, the music is right. And then after that we're going to check how the rhythm, they can do the break we need to make the music sound the way we got the stops and (claps hands) the way they're supposed to stop (laughs).

Going to Mexico

[While I was with] Sensación somebody by the name of Ninón Mondéjar asked me if I wanted to go to Mexico to play with Orquesta América. Ninón Mondéjar was a güiro player, he wasn't a musician. But he's the one that started the Orquesta América with Enrique Jorrín, Antonio Sánchez, Alex Sosa on the piano. He was the person who used to do the bookkeeping and the contracts and those type of things. Jorrín was the violin player of that orchestra. Jorrín was the creator of the cha cha cha, he was the first violin of that Orquesta América.

I think the problem with Enrique Jorrín and Ninón Mondéjar was this: Enrique Jorrín was a technical musician, incredible writing, arranging. He was the one [who] did all these tunes like *Engañadora*, bunch of good tunes. And then from one moment to the other, that Ninón Mondéjar sees that the cha cha cha was so popular, that Ninón Mondéjar starts saying that he was the creator of the cha cha cha, which he's not. And then Jorrín, he says, "Oh, yeah, you're gonna say that you're the creator of the cha cha when I did *Engañadora*, all those tunes that have been popular. No, man, I'm quitting this band and I'm gonna make my own band." And then Jorrín did charanga with trompetas, and that's it. [The] disagreement between Ninón Mondéjar and Enrique Jorrín was that Ninón Mondéjar tried to say to the magazines in Cuba, like *Bohemia* and *Carteles*, that he was the creator of the cha cha cha, which [he] was not. All the musicians that knew about the music, knew that Ninón Mondéjar wasn't a musician. The doctor of music was Enrique Jorrín, who was the one and the only one [that] created, did the cha cha cha.

Jorrín made his own band and then Ninón Mondéjar was talking, he got no violin players. Ninón Mondéjar was having problems with some musicians who couldn't get used to the weather or the high [altitudes] of Mexico. They said, "Ni-nón, we cannot take it, man, we gotta come back to Havana." So Ninón went (claps hands) right away to Havana and he gotta find some musicians to finish whatever he got.

So Ninón went to me and there, right away I accepted the proposition. Imagine that was Enrique Jorrín, the best, and Ninón Mondéjar—I was a kid and he comes to me—*me*—to replace Enrique Jorrín, the best one! And then I went to Orquesta América to Mexico, I stayed with América in Mexico for two years. [Flutist] Gon-zalo Fernandez went with me, and Chucho, the timbal [player] we used to use in Sensación, he went with me, too.

We traveled all over Mexico. From Mexico [City] we went to Veracruz, Aca-pulco, Tampico down to around Guatemala. You know, we were traveling around Central America. We used to live in Luis Moilla 87 in Mexico City. That's where

Hermanos Rigual used to live, Enrique Jorrín used to live there, some of the musicians from [Orquesta] América.

We used to play with América at El Burro, El Pigalle, El Afro. That's big. These are high-class dancehalls, this is no joke—incredible, incredible! They've got the band playing for people dancing and they've got the shows. Sometimes they've got Marcantonio Muñiz, they've got different big musicians and singers from there.

América did eleven different movies. Rolando Lozano is playing in those movies. Rolando was with the band at that time. That was in the beginning when they get there, when the cha cha cha was real big in Mexico. Ninón Mondéjar, Félix Reína too. These incredible musicians, like Enrique Jorrín. These and all the top musicians, incredible. Félix Reína: he was the second violin there. [Reína took over Fajardo's band when Fajardo emigrated.]

Mexican people, they're very enthusiastic for the Cuban music; they call it tropical music. So they've usually got some style, like American style and rock and this and that. But when they see the Cuban rhythm they're calling it música tropical, you know. And they're crazy about dancing and asking and seeing those instruments because they don't usually have those types of instruments there. They really hear a lot of trumpets but not flute and violin. They got the violin, the violin is very popular for the mariachi but not with the vamp we use and the rhythm we've got there (laughs). Like [it] is like a train, you know (laughs).

Returning to Havana

I went back to Havana, [to play again with] Sensación and I played a little bit with Fajardo in Cuba too. Once in a while, you know. When I came back from Mexico to Havana, I felt like I didn't belong there. You know the people in Mexico—incredible! I felt like a real artist. I went back to Havana and I wasn't the same person.

Communism in Cuba at that time was under the table. We didn't really know what was going on. I could see that something bad was going to happen over there. They were putting bombs in the street. There were a lot of accidents and people were very scared. There was no security. You couldn't go in the streets at night. Anything could happen. Castro's people were doing that against the Batista government. Very dangerous.

Leaving Cuba and Joining El Nuevo Ritmo

At the beginning of 1958 I was doing those radio station broadcasts. Everybody in Cuba was doing that. So I saw Rudy Calzado, and I said, "If you have a chance to play in that group [Orquesta Nuevo Ritmo, also called New Cuban Rhythm] you play with in Chicago, brother, I'm *down. Now!*" Rudy, right away he calls Armando [Sánchez] and Nicolas "Cuco" Martínez. And they need a violin player and they say, "OK, Rudy, we're gonna send you the ticket and we're gonna send the ticket to Pupi, too, because we need a violin player here." The violin player with Orquesta Nuevo Ritmo was Elizardo Aroche, the one [who] was in Mexico after Jorrín finished, with me over there. Arocha was a concert musician from [the] Jalapa Symphony. He died a few years ago.

Catalino Rolón, that's the person [who] brought me to here, to this country, to that band. Catalino Rolón is the uncle of René López. He's the one [who] really sent me the ticket. Catalino Rolón, in the Palladium he was the person [who] was in charge of the setting of the groups and everything and bringing musicians from Cuba. And he's the one [who] knows about the Spanish market, what's going on about, putting Tito Rodríguez, Tito Puente, Machito, Vicentico [Valdés], Alfredito Valdés and bringing Arsenio Rodríguez. All those groups, Marcelino Guerra, even Mongo Santamaría. I saw when one of the times I was playing with Sensación in Cuba, Catalino, I saw Catalino Rolón in Cuba. Yeah, he used to go to Cuba. I even saw Tito Puente in Cuba, too. All these people, they have to go sometimes to do business and find groups. You know, at that time he could buy the group when he didn't have to go through the government or anything. At that time he goes to the leader of the band or whatever: "Hey, you want to go to the United States?" "Yes," so on and so on. "OK, how much you want?" "Oh, two thousand," whatever. "OK, send me the contract, send me the money and send me the business and then I go to the American Consul to get the visa." That's how you used to do it. Catalino was very much involved in making that stuff happen. He was incredible. This [man] was like René López: (pats chest) this was a good heart. Believe me, I cannot express myself exactly the way he was: he was [an] incredible person. He's the best.

When I got to Chicago and I saw how cold was Chicago, I say "What, excuse me!" (laughs). Oh my God, believe me, imagine Chicago in November! It snows, and I've never seen snow in my life. Not even in Mexico, in the what do you call it, in the high mountains in Mexico that they've got a little bit of snow. That Chicago was incredible, November 18, 1959. I cannot forget. I came with a silk suit from Cuba. Nice looking, you know—like a pimp. The band was incredible, you know. Armando Sánchez started that group with "Cuco"—Nicolás Martínez, the bass player from Melodias del Cuarenta. And Armando Sánchez the conga player and René "Látigo" Hernández on the piano, Rolando Lozano on the flute, Victor Venegas on the bass. He's from Chicago.

We played together with Aragón at the Palladium at 53rd and Broadway in New York. Believe me—you know, I don't want to talk no more, you know. When people saw this band together with Aragón, Aragón is a band that [is] playing every day and we play together at the Palladium. Nobody was looking even at Aragón, was looking Nuevo Ritmo of Cuba—incredible! And everybody knows that, it's not that I'm trying to say that we were better. [It's] that, you know how the people are. Aragón is strict there, what they play there, they don't go out, like what is on the paper is there. And Richard Egües is doing whatever he gotta do—they're playing for Richard Egües, that's the way (laughs) Aragón looks like. And Nuevo Ritmo was different; this was like a show band. René Hernández in the piano, moving the way he was doing. And Rudy Calzado's singing and dancing. Me, I was moving, too (laughs). But at this point Nuevo Ritmo of Cuba and Aragón at the Palladium— everybody knows what happened that night over there (laughs), you know? Aragón was playing and OK, it was OK, Aragón, OK (claps hands), they clap and everything. But when New Rhythm of Cuba played there at that time people really almost died. Believe me, you know?

Working for Mongo

And then we went down to L.A. When we were in L.A., we were doing bad. And then Mongo Santamaría talked to me. He said, "Pupi, I got the contract with Fantasy Records, I need you to write some arrangements for me because we're gonna start." And then that's when we did the *Sabroso* album for Mongo, that I did all that music for him. Then *Para Ti* and all those tunes—I did about 48 arrangements for Mongo and Fantasy Records. Those records Mongo did, one album they're calling *Sabroso, Más Sabroso*, so on and so on. It's about four albums, it's a session there he did for Fantasy Records. So when Mongo did those records he was playing with Cal Tjader, meaning that he was traveling through Chicago to Baltimore, to New York. So he was seeing Federico Pagani. Right there Federico Pagani I think offered Mongo—"Hey Mongo, why you don't make the charanga with Pupi, Rolando and those people, Cuco and those?" And then that's how I came back, and I met Federico Pagani when we came to the Caravana Club, 442 East 149th [Street]. And from there we made the band with Mongo; we work about a year or so with Mongo. And then after that Mongo went to that *Watermelon Man*, he changed the sound. I played with him for two or three years. And then from there I did the first album with Tico Records.

Cubans in New York Before the Revolution

Cuban people like New York a lot. A lot of tourists, even people from Cuba, they used to come here to see the baseball World Series. A lot of Cubans been living here since the 1940s and before that. And a lot of people from Cuba, they used to come only to see the World Series, baseball World Series. It was hard for a Cuban guy to get a visa. Because you need somebody here to put some money down as a security or whatever, immigration guy requires, you know. The ticket used to cost three or four hundred dollars anyhow. And you couldn't come here as a tourist and stay here—no way! Immigration will get you and send you back to Cuba. And if you came here with no resident green card, you had to get married. And by the time you finished your papers already the gig was over.

Catalino says to Mr. Hyman at the Palladium (that's his boss)—I'm taking a guess, you know: "Mr. Hyman, I'm bringing some Cuban guy from Havana, OK? I'm gonna use the Palladium and so and so, and the plane for this to send." "It's OK, OK, Catalino, do it"—because Catalino got the green light to do everything. Catalino was the one who did the papers but Mr. Hyman was the one putting [his] bank book for me. Because I came as a tourist and I stay. With a work visa, I came with a work visa. Lucky that I came in 1959. I did it, I got it by luck. I was a lucky person because I'm not even thinking about anything.

Becoming a Flutist

I found out that I needed a flute player. I couldn't get Richard Egües, I couldn't get Rolando Lozano, he lived down in L.A. I said to myself: "I gotta practice the flute!" And then I became a flute player, five-key, eighteenth century—that's a difficult, hard instrument, you know? So that's how you gotta make it and you gotta do it if you really want to do it the way we do it in Cuba. I became a flute player just because I cannot get nobody else. I took [up] the flute about 1963, '62, '64, '65. With that flute you gotta find somebody that knows the old positions. Johnny Pacheco gave me the positions of that flute. And I started studying the mouthpiece (makes the flute embouchure and blows), how to conduct the air for almost one or two months until my lip was getting—and every time I put my mouthpiece to my lips I can get that sound, the same note, and right there with the other part I was studying the position. And then I wrote my father to send me a book for that flute, a very old book from Tulou, that's the system for it. [Tulou was a famous nineteenth-century French flute virtuoso who wrote concert music and studies.] There I find a lot of positions and a lot of what they're calling *tranquillas*, like tricks, how you do the trills. And there I find, you know, some technique about the flute, how they're writing. [Sounds an octave lower than written.] All these Cuban flute players studied [that book] for that type of flute.

In Cuba there was a problem to find instruments, to find an instrument to play. The classical flute players [often had cheap] metal flutes. They can play with a metal flute, they got the flute. Like Richard Egües now. He got a metal flute, you know, cheap, you know, it's cheap. But at least he got one. He said, "Pupi, I'm playing too many dances with the wood flute. It's too much, it's too hard, you know? So that's why I have to find myself a way not to work so much. So that's why I'm playing sometimes with the metal flute." And the other problem we got is that when this flute gets broken or cracked, it's a problem. You cannot replace parts. Those flutes, they're from Paris. That's the people [who] did this flute. Martin, Buffet, and another one, La Mosca. A lot of people wrote to Paris asking if they could get a flute like that. And they say that in the last war the bombs destroyed the companies and they got no way. You gotta find it in a pawnshop or someplace.

Like I said: in those years, 1930s or around the 1940s how you're gonna find a metal flute in Cuba? Was not in there, even in those years it was not in there like that. Only the people [who] have the metal flute were the people [who] used to play in the classical. Maybe they got money, they wrote to some company in United States, they got the instrument. But the other people in the street, they're real poor people, you know, people that—and sometimes they play one or three dances a year only. Used to make for the New Year's Eve $20, $15. So how you're gonna buy a flute that costs over a hundred dollars?

Fania All-Stars

Ah, one day, [it] was something. I lent Pacheco some flute and the flute got lost (laughs) and then they was calling me back and forth about this thing. And then from one moment to the other when I was living at 370 West 51st I heard that somebody was calling me to the window. It was Alex Masucci saying, "Hey, Pupi, Gerry, he wants you to go to the office." And then I went to the office when they were at 57th Street. And then Gerry asked me, "Hey, you want to go with me to Africa?" and then I said "OK, man, no problem."[24]

I just doubled with the trombone parts. And after we finished whatever *efecto*, you know, I just keep, I just forget about what I'm playing and all the beginning part of the tune. And I keep in the rhythm section, I've been making my own system to play with the Fania All-Stars. As a matter of fact I do the intro, I do all the body part of the tunes with the trombones. When I get to the montuno instead of me keeping with the trombone section I listen to the piano or whatever, I've got my part there with the piano chords and I'm vamping with the rhythm section. That's how I make my arrangement. I mean—hey, since the first day I have to look out about how I'm gonna play with this type of instrumentation. In other words I look ridiculous or they're gonna say "Hey, Pupi, you gotta stay home because you're not filling in, you're not doing the job" or "You really messed up." You know what I'm saying?

I've been making a little bit of money with Gerry. I've been working for, like, Larry Harlow, other people there. I've been recording, yeah, they've been saying "Pupi, I need you to . . ." You see that solo from *Manuela, Pupi Toca La Manuela*, that I play the violin there and other people there—yeah. Sometimes they've got some violin *efecto*, whatever, they've been calling me there. Hey, that's why I don't try to fight with the man. Instead of me going with another person I try to stay with him. Because in this year I figured out, I say, "Hey, with this amount of chicken, you know (laughs), I've been making out," you know? Believe me. And then I cannot spit on top of my face, you know, and not give the credit to that. [Bookkeeper] Victor Gallo, Gerry Masucci, even Pacheco, you know. Even Pacheco's been calling me for jobs that sometimes I cannot make and I feel sorry. One time he called me for Africa, I want to go and I cannot do it. At that time I don't even have the papers, really.

When I got this with the Fania, I decided this Broadway and this Novel and Sublime and this band that I started in New York—believe it or not, all these people worked for me. But when I got this with the Fania and I've been recording all the time, every time I say "Masucci, I got the music," he's been recording me. So why am I gonna keep a band with some weak musicians that are not playing what I can play on the record with good musicians, when I've been doing the best, recording these records. And besides that making much, much more money with Masucci doing this, traveling, than I've been doing with—OK, it's true, I've been taking a chance on this playing (laughs), to kill myself. But at least I let people in Miami that want to see Pupi, people in Paris, people in Africa, 22 times, me in Africa, thank you. You know? So this is what I'm happy about, my career in the music, that I know that everybody knows Pupi Legarreta, thank you. You know, that's—I'm happy about that. If I die tomorrow I know that I'm not some star like some people are calling me, I know that. But [the] only thing I know is that they will remember Pupi because Pupi's been passing through all these locations, believe it or not.

Afro-Cuban Religions and Musicians

The musicians like me or even my teacher or El Niño Prodigio, we have no association with the [cult drummers]. Nothing. Especially with Abakuá. That's a religion that we don't even see their things. I don't think that Mongo, Patato or Armando were that involved in [the Afro-Cuban religions]. These people were always playing dance music in Cuba. This is my opinion. I never saw Mongo or Armando Peraza doing that type of music. They know that as a foundation because they're from Cuba like me. We feel these things and we know what they're doing.

But we're not into that. That's a different type of musician. We don't even see them when they play. They do that in places—when you're not in the religion you can't even go inside to see those things.

Playing Charanga on the Violin

One of the problems of the violin is that many violin players, they don't have too much rhythm to keep steady the beat or whatever vamp is there. But if you're playing with other violins it's better [if] you play the same music. This way you will get together and you will blend with the other violin players. The only thing— you have to push where the rhythm is and keep it there.

The pressure we use in the popular music is a lot more than how much pressure you use in the classic music, you know. In the classic music you got thirty violins there, sitting in there. Everybody is playing the *efecto* because you've got all the ones reinforcing. The violin is not a strong instrument. For you to have a strong sound with the violin you need at least 15 or 20. And so imagine us in the charanga, when we've got two or three how we gotta keep the *efecto* there, up- and down- bow, you know. So you can get some idea of what I'm saying.

Improvisation

If you cannot hear the harmony you never improvise. I could mention some names of musicians who could never improvise, because they don't have the ear. If you don't have the ear you don't know how those chords are going to go. You don't have the foundation of how harmony moves.

Current Musical Plans

Currently I play with Siglo Veinte. [Like several other bands based in the United States, this group's name comes from a prerevolutionary ensemble. Siglo Veinte was a danzón group of the 1920s.] Last week I went to record with Humberto Corredor, a Colombian who works with Sergio Bofil and this record company, Guajira Records. It was old-style Cuban music. They don't want any new styles of music. They say, "Pupi, we need the old-style Cuban music because we cannot sell [the newer styles] to Africa and, especially, Colombia and Venezuela." They just want the old style of Cuban music. I don't really feel too good about that. There's got to be some change.

9

The Trombone Man: A Cuban Jazz Musician in the United States

Cuban musicians have been coming to the United States since before World War II. In the postwar years, a handful of Cuba's greatest percussions such as Mongo Santamaría, Francisco Aguabella, Armando Peraza and Cándido Camero made their way to the States. Their profound influence on stateside Cuban music belied their small number. Around the time of the Cuban Revolution, what had been a trickle of Cuban musicians became somewhat of a minor flood. And then it nearly stopped. After the 1962 Bay of Pigs incident, Castro suspended air service to the United States. In 1965, with little advance notice, he allowed Cubans who had close relatives in the United States to leave the island by boat from the port of Camarioca. This time, it was the U.S. State Department who cut off the escape route. As an alternative, President Johnson negotiated a "Memorandum of Understanding" with Cuba in which Castro agreed to resume air flights for Cubans with close relatives in the United States. About 300,000 Cubans came to the United States from 1965 to 1973, when Castro cut off the hemorrhaging flow of Cubans from his country.[1] Few musicians came during this period, especially since draft-age men were excluded from the freedom flights. In the late 1960s through the early 1970s, a few musicians who had fled to Mexico and elsewhere rerooted themselves in the United States, but the exodus of Cuban musicians appeared to be finished.

In the early years of Castro's revolution, the arts were under pressure to conform to the expectations and demands of the young government. Afro-Cuban influences were closely watched because the Cuban government viewed all religious activity with suspicion. Castro and his associates were troubled by racial orientation, which they considered inappropriate in a worker's society. In the national arts schools, any music other than Western classical was prohibited by the Eastern European faculty:

When the students tried to play Cuban music, they would be admonished and even punished. They'd lose weekend privileges . . . It became a clandestine activity. This ended years ago, but it was a weird phase and during that time the kids had to do everything hidden in their dorm rooms. They would say: "Tonight there's a *timba* in room number nine!" Or "We're going to have a *timba*, tonight. We're going to *timbiar*!"[2]

Artists had to be careful to hide their American influences. Musicians who played jazz were accused of being pro-Yankee.[3] By the middle of the 1970s, the government realized that fostering artistic expression would shed a favorable light on Cuba, especially for European and American youths who already had taken the bearded Che Guevara as one of their folk heroes. Under the administration of Armando Hart Davalos, the newly formed Ministry of Culture (instituted in 1976) worked to unshackle artistic expression. Music gained new respect as a means of promoting Cuban culture throughout the world.[4] Musicians were allowed to play jazz and rock without fear of being denounced. Afro-Cuban culture was recognized for its centrality to Cuban culture. In fact, the government realized that promoting Afro-Cuban culture was an easy wasy to reach out to dark-skinned Cubans and, at the same time, diminish the pervasive influence of Castro's chief enemy, the United States.

Cuban jazz thrived during the 1970s. Irakere, the band led by pianist "Chucho" Valdés that featured Paquito D'Rivera and Arturo Sandoval, performed throughout the world. In 1978, the Cuban government permitted them to perform at Carnegie Hall. The live concert recording won Irakere a Grammy award in 1978.

In the same year, the Cuban government initiated talks with a group of Cuban exiles. The *Diálogo* of November 1978 led the way toward the release of thousands of political prisoners. More important, it lifted travel restrictions for the exiles to visit their friends and families in Cuba. The exiles, labeled *gusanos* ("worms") by the Castro government, were now greeted as *mariposas* ("butterflies") who flew back to Cuba with gifts in tow. The sight of so many well-off Cuban Americans on the island had an unforeseen consequence for Castro: it spread political dissatisfaction and created a powerful desire in the hearts of many Cubans for a better way of life.[5]

Cuban jazz musicians were probably more disaffected than other Cubans. With more and more glimpses at the world just 90 miles away, they surely were tired of being the best-of-the-best on a poor Caribbean island. The Cuban government recognized their achievements and, in comparison to most Cubans, treated them well. But perhaps as a result of this same treatment, Cuban jazz musicians bristled when the government rejected their efforts to develop artistically. Of course, the only way to do *that* properly was to move off the island. While Cuba was the center of Afro-Cuban popular music, New York was the center of the jazz world. Cubans jazz musicians knew that they could never hope to reach an international audience without securing a New York address.

In 1980, a Havana bus driver rammed his vehicle through the gates of the Peruvian embassy and demanded political asylum. A set of events transpired that eventually led to the *Mariel* boat lift. A number of Cuban jazz musicians such as Ignacio Berroa left Cuba at that time. D'Rivera followed a year later. While on tour in Spain, he sought asylum at the American Embassy. A decade later, Arturo Sandoval came, and soon afterward trombonist Juan Pablo Torres.

JUAN PABLO TORRES

Trombone virtuoso Juan Pablo Torres was born in 1946 on the northeastern coast of Cuba in Oriente Province. He became well known as a member of the Orquesta Cubana de Música Moderna, the band that also brought fame to Arturo Sandoval, Paquito d'Rivera and Chucho Valdés. During the 1970s, Torres was a producer at the Cuban national recording company EGREM (Enterprise of Recordings and Musical Editions). In 1979, he produced and directed a famous *descarga* ("jam session") for Areito, the EGREM recording label. He dubbed the ensemble of all-star musicians *Las Estrellas de Areito* (the Areito All-Stars). Twenty years later, the recordings were reissued and distributed worldwide to great acclaim. In 1984, Torres went to Italy to record music written by Astor Piazzolla for the film *Richard IV*, directed by Marco Belocchio. In 1992, Torres and his group, which included his wife, Elsa Lazo Torres, traveled to Spain to perform there. The Cuban government's policy at the time was that only members of the Communist Party could leave the island with their spouses. In Torres's case, the government was apparently unaware that Ms. Lazo was Torres's wife, so they were able to leave together. At the end of the tour, the Béla Bartók conservatory located in Zaragoza proposed that Torres and his wife remain to teach. When he asked the Cuban officials if he could stay for another contract, he was told that he had to return with the rest of the group. In that moment, Torres grabbed the opportunity to escape Cuba. After living in Spain for a year, Torres and Lazo moved to Miami. Since relocating to the United States, Torres has played for President Clinton at his inauguration, was featured at the Olympics in Atlanta, Georgia, and has participated in several concerts at Carnegie Hall and Radio City Music Hall. He has performed with numerous legendary artists such as Dizzy Gillespie, Gato Barbieri, Israel Cachao López, Tito Puente,

Steve Turre, Randy Brecker, Giovanni Hidalgo and Mario Bauzá. A few years ago Torres and Lazo moved to Union City, New Jersey, where they are neighbors with Paquito D'Rivera. *Trombone Man*, Torres's North American debut album, came out on the Tropijazz label in 1995. The album was produced by D'Rivera, who also plays alto saxophone and clarinet on the recording. Torres uses the name "The Trombone Man" as a kind of trademark identification. At the conclusion of our conversation, Torres played me some of his recordings that were scheduled for release in 2000. They made clear that Torres deserves to call himself "The Trombone Man."

Torres is good friends with the Buena Vista Social Club band, several of whom were members of Las Estrellas de Areito. When they came to the United States in 1998 for a concert at Carnegie Hall, Torres arranged to have them perform with him at the Hard Grove Cafe, a Jersey City diner where Torres hosted a Thursday evening jam session. Later on that evening, they recorded a session with Torres.

I interviewed Torres at his home in Union City, an enclave of Cuban Americans for nearly 40 years. Torres spoke to me in a clearly understood Spanish that I have been told is typical in his part of the island, the northeastern coast.

I was born in Oriente in Puerto Padre. There was a band there, a municipal band. My Dad played in the band. He played the trumpet, bombardino [euphonium] and trombone. I was surrounded by music ever since I was born. At age 10 or 11 I was in the band playing an instrument that's like a soprano bombardino but a small one. Then I went to the bombardino, but what I really wanted to play was the trombone. When the trombone seat became empty, I took it. I was 14 at the time.

I studied with my father, but he didn't teach me much because there was no learning manual for my instrument. I had to send away to Havana for it. I got the trombone method, but what happened is that a clarinetist in the band and I learned trombone through the clarinet method. I was basically self-taught; I didn't have a teacher.

A group from our town entered a competition in Havana and won. We went on a tour to the USSR. When I returned, I entered the Escuela Nacional de Arte. Arturo [Sandoval] was already there. I studied with Antonio Liñares, who was then the trombone soloist in the National Symphony Orchestra.

The musicians who in the past have played in symphony orchestras played in Cuban orchestras as well. My teacher comes from popular orchestras, as does Arturo's. Even the soloist from the National Symphony Orchestra, Luis Escalante, was a trumpeter who played both kinds of music.

I don't believe that the reason for the high quality of musicians since the Castro revolution is due to the Soviet influence. In the area of string instruments, yes, the Russian influence was very strong. The brass instruments are an American school; we are so close to the Americans that the wind instruments and percussion have evolved a lot in Cuba.

In the 1970s, we weren't allowed to study popular music or jazz in school. We music students had to go out to jazz clubs at night, and to play in those clubs to learn the music. Only recently has Cuban popular music been added to the curriculum. I was one of the ones who organized and brought this into the school curriculum. However, the specialists in folkloric music were in the street and in the CFN (*Conjunto Folklórico Nacional*, National Folkloric Ensemble of Cuba). People who wanted to learn Cuban music would go as they still do today, to study privately in the musicians' houses. People from all over the world go to Cuba to study with [percussionist] Changuito, for example. Changuito gives private lessons. Learning percussion in a conservatory has nothing to do with playing the tumbadoras. The conga and tumbadora are learned by ear. In Cuba, the percussionists were the ones who couldn't read. Everybody else could read music, because we always had the town bands. During my time in Cuba, the pay scale was different than it is here. The leader got the most, then, the instrumentalists. The percussionists got paid the least.

In Cuba, music is organized by the state; musicians received a salary from the government. This was my experience as a Cuban musician; I'm not saying whether it is good or bad. The government made artistic evaluations—collective and individual ones. For example, an orchestra would be graded as a group and given a category—first category, second or third category. The same system would be applied to the individual musicians as well. In an orchestra there would be different levels or categories of musicians. To be in the first category you had to have knowledge of theory, harmony, and music history, and be able to read music. As a general rule, the most "popular" musicians aren't always the best. The ones with the highest level are trying to make more complex music, and obviously this isn't always the most well-liked music. The most "popular" has more acceptance, and people constantly wanted to hear it. The classification system brought about a contradiction: the "best" is not the most "popular." The government made exceptions for certain orchestras like Orquesta Aragón, because of their longevity and popularity. Aragón, the Orquesta Cubana de Música Moderna, and the symphony orchestra automatically received the highest rating. Besides, *we* were the ones who evaluated or rated the musicians. Until the end of 1991, this rating system was still happening. I really don't know what has been going on over the last seven years in Cuba because I have no information. We have family there still and we talk on the phone, but I can't say about how things are in Cuban music now.

I was in the Escuela Nacional de Arte for only one year—from 1966 to 1967. In 1967, the Orquesta Cubana de Música Moderna was formed and I began playing with them: Arturo, Paquito, Chucho, Carlos Emilio, all those people. At the same time I played with Pacho Alonso's band. I always loved Cuban popular music, and within the orchestra I formed my own group: Algo Nuevo. So out of the Orquesta Cubana de Música Moderna came Irakere and my group. I always wanted to do my music within the idiom of Cuban popular music. I think that what I did was Latin jazz. Since I did instrumental music, the singer in my group was the trombone. Irakere dedicated itself more to Afro-Cuban jazz. I dedicated myself to researching Cuban popular music and bringing it within a concert format. We played in a lot of lowlife dives. We played in Mexico and in Europe. For one year, we played in a show at the Hotel Nacional in Havana. Also, we appeared in a film called *Noche de Carnaval.*

Along with the political orientation, there was a musical orientation. I wasn't regarded as a jazz musician because in those days if you were a jazz musician, that's all you did. I played only once in the jazz festival because the organizer didn't think of me. My music was within the Latin jazz idiom, even though at the time that name, "Latin jazz," didn't exist in Cuba.

The other work I did was with EGREM. I was the founder of the production group. I produced a lot of records—Los Van Van, Omara Portuando, Chapotín, Helena Burke, Miriam Ramos, lots of people. The famous Estrellas de Areito arrived at a time when no other group existed that really had commercial success with Cuban music. Raoul Diomandé was the executive producer and I was the musical director. EGREM asked me to pick the best musicians from the best orchestras. The idea was to do something like the Fania All-Stars. Among the musicians were Arturo, Chappotín, Jorge Varona, Manuel "El Guajiro" Mirabal, Fabián García, Amadito Valdés, Filiberto Sánchez, Jesús Rubalcaba, El Niño Rivera, Paquito, etc. Well, I think that at that time a record was made that can never be made again. So many have died, and others of us went abroad. Those that remained in Cuba made Buena Vista Social Club. When you hear *Estrellas de Areito*, when you hear the job I did with arrangements and musical direction, it was very important because I was able to draw out the best from each of the musicians. I think that one should speak about this record because it gave a push to this kind of music in Cuba. It wasn't a success in Cuba though, because they never played it on the radio. Because the criteria with which they give radio play has to do with popular taste!

[I was told by a prominent Latin musician that many Cuban immigrants have problems adapting to the system here. I asked Juan Pablo Torres to talk about this.]

Yes, it's a great contradiction. Because of a lack of demand or a market, the musicians in Cuba have developed *themselves* a great deal. Because we *do* have a market here, we have not advanced as much. A good example is NG La Banda, a group with an incredible pool of talent. Over here it's difficult to achieve that sort of level and maintain it. It's very difficult to rehearse, because you have to rent the studio and pay the musicians to rehearse. One must juggle between these two extremes: one has to find a way to make *good* music that is commercial. If it's good and not commercial, it doesn't sell. The musicians that come here contribute to the growth of the music because in Cuba they could dedicate themselves to music without having to sell themselves to "this one" or "that one."

Latin jazz needs to be understood and heard more. I think the CDs have to embrace popular taste more without diminishing the music itself. The Latin musicians [being featured] are the same ones—Tito Puente, Eddie Palmieri, Paquito—but there are some new ones from Venezuela, Columbia, Puerto Rico and Cuba. There have always been Cubans [in Latin jazz]. Latin jazz is not commercial music; it belongs in festivals, concerts. The Latin jazz musicians of the highest caliber support themselves on jazz festivals. But it's very hard to fill an auditorium with a concert of Latin jazz, unless that concert is marketed as such. It's hard to get money from the sponsors for a Latin jazz concert. It's difficult.

I've played here with Dizzy, Steve Turre, Tito Puente. I play with the Tropijazz All-Stars, which is put out by RMM. I have two CDs coming out that I did with "El Guajiro" Mirabal, Cachaito, Amadito. In July 1999, I did a tour in Europe called Jazz in Clave with Chucho Valdés, Giovanni Hidalgo, Claudio Roditi. In

February 2000, I'm going to do the most important CD of my life. I'm doing it with a German record company called Thermidor. On it will be Steve Turre, Robin Eubanks, Claudio Roditi, Ed Simon, Giovanni Hidalgo and Horacio "El Negro" Hernández. In June I've got a concert at Colgate University. I do trombone clinics, but as an Afro-Cuban musician. There are a lot of jazz trombonists who give clinics. I am in a better position as an Afro-Cuban trombonist than as a jazz trombonist. My work now is with an invention of mine that measures the air flow. It is meant to control the column of air.

[I asked Torres about the pendant he wears.]

It's an amulet. It doesn't make a noise, it's a turtle. I'm not interested in African deities. In Puerto Padre, the village I was born in, there is a tradition which is guajira, not African. The only African influence [on the guajira tradition] comes from Haiti, not [directly] from Africa. The slaves who cut sugar cane there were Haitian.

THE TROMBONE MAN'S MUSIC

The Estrellas de Areito recordings were issued in the United States 20 years after the original recording date as a double CD package with a 48-page booklet containing notes about the sessions, photographs and extensively transcribed and translated lyrics. The recordings, titled *Los Heroes*, were produced by Nick Gold and World Circuit, the group responsible for the Buena Vista Social Club and its spin-offs such as the Afro-Cuban All-Stars. *Los Heroes* is a masterpiece of Cuban popular music and a memorial to great old Cuban musicians, several of whom died shortly after. Pianist Rubén González, who played on several of the recordings, retired from music a few years later. At the time, he never could have dreamed that his career would be revived more than a decade later when he was picked to be a member of the Buena Vista Social Club. He is now an international star.

Juan Pablo Torres produced the music and contributed sketches that could function as fills or bridges between solos. On a few selections, he played trombone in the brass section and took a few stunning improvised solos. The ad-hoc arrangements are a case study for anyone interested in creating music with limited elements. Jesús "Aguaje" Ramos was the other trombonist in the Estrellas group. He recalled what the recording sessions were like:

The arrangements were real shorthand—eight bars, the brass section and a coda. That really was improvisation! Juan Pablo would write something down and say, "We'll play like this here." Then another musician would say, "I've got an idea, let's try this" but when you start and you improvise you just do whatever comes to your ear. He made the work easy and when you're relaxed, you always get good results. It took about a week. Everything was very spontaneous. I don't think we'd ever be able to create an atmosphere like that again.[6]

Torres wrote two songs for the session, *U-La-La* and *Prepara Los Cueros*. Both are typical descarga lyrics—just a few words to provide a framework for the singers to add their spur-of-the-moment impressions of the music as it was unfolding under Torres's direction. "Listen to the flute, how good it is! Melquiades, Melquiades: That's right!" Teresa Garcia Caturla encourages the flute soloist, Melquiades Fundora during the song, *U-La-La*. *Prepara los Cueros* ("Prepare the drums") has just two lines of lyrics: "Prepare the drums for a jam. The rhythm's great, I want to dance." After that, the singers provide a running commentary on the music: "It's time for Chapotín . . . Here comes Arturo," and so on.

The first CD opens with *Póngase para las cosas* ("Take good note"). The lyrics were written in response to the worldwide growth of salsa and its promotion as a form of Hispanic music developed in New York. At the time, it seemed like the world was forgetting about Cuban popular music. Prerevolutionary popular music and the stars who made it were no longer in fashion, especially in Cuba. So *Póngase para las cosas* is a warning to those who forget the Cuban roots of salsa. The *coro* boldly states: "Take note: *el son* still reigns supreme. If they tell you it's salsa, it's a lie—it's *son!*" The lead singers, Pio Leyva and Tito Gómez, make their case with much passion.

Pio Leyva takes charge after the first *coro* statement to praise Raoul Diomandé, the Ivory Coast record producer who inspired the creation of Las Estrellas. Next, he extolls the famous soneros such as Abelardo Barroso "the falsetto" and his descendents Roberto Faz, Cheo Marquetti and Beny Moré. Then he gives a nod in the direction of two Estrellas participants, the singers Miguelito Cuní and Tito Gómez. The latter also sings on *Póngase*. Pio Leyva closes his five stanzas of mostly improvised text with a Yoruba expression, *Erein aba morum*. Leyva is directly within the sonero tradition of announcing his pedigree as someone with deep roots in Afro-Cuban tradition, someone from *el monte adentro*.

After Leyva finishes, Tito Gomez grabs the microphone, and the two singers engage in another sonero tradition: a battle of wits. After the singing come solos by Miguel "Brindis" Barbón, whose nickname comes after the famous nineteenth-century Afro-Cuban classical violinist Brindis de Sala. Barbón was also called *el niño prodigio*—"the child prodigy."

Torres gives himself a chance to shine on a few tracks. My favorite is *Fefita*, an old danzón written by José Urfé that Torres arranged for his trombone along with trumpeter Arturo Sandoval and rhythm section. After the introductory section comes a montuno section in which Torres shows his ability to improvise at breakneck speeds.

10

Juan-Carlos Formell

After the American-made Buena Vista Social Club, Los Van Van is the most famous band to develop in Cuba since the revolution. Because Los Van Van has been flourishing under the eyes of the Castro government for over 30 years, the group is perceived to be the official band of the Cuban Revolution. Juan Formell is the founder of the group—its arranger, chief songwriter and bassist. In a recent interview Juan Formell appears to want to distance himself from Castro, but in the past he has, at the least, performed songs with political messages shared by his government. He is considered to be the most famous person in Cuba after Fidel. So when his son, Juan-Carlos Formell, surfaced from anonymity as a recording artist and Grammy nominee in the United States, a new chapter in the Cuban saga was revealed.

Born in 1964, Juan-Carlos was the first child of Juan Formell and Natalia Alfonso. His mother was a cabaret entertainer.[1] When he was just three weeks old, he was sent to be raised by his father's parents, María and Francisco. Francisco Formell had been a respected zarzuela conductor and composer and the arranger for Ernesto Lecuona's group, Lecuona's Cuban Boys. There is a family story that when Juan-Carlos was born, his grandfather went to the hospital to see his new grandson. Seeing the baby, he announced that he had the hands of a musician. By the time Juan-Carlos was born, Francisco was out of favor with the Castro government for being too associated with the past. Juan-Carlos was raised in poverty in a remote part of Havana. When Juan-Carlos was still an infant, Francisco died, but through his book collection, Francisco continued to influence his grandson. Formell remembers one book in particular: a book about Cuban music.

A new-man entered Formell's grandmother's life. María's new husband was a seaman who rescued wounded animals. A large tortoise was invited into their little home, and the animal slept under Juan-Carlos's bed. During the weekends, Formell visited his parents, where he was able to watch some of Cuba's best musicians enjoy themselves in informal performances and jam sessions. Formell began his first instrument, the guitar, at the age of seven. He learned by watching the great Cuban guitarists playing in his mother's house. Formell also learned to play the bass, his father's instrument. His teacher was symphonic bassist Andrés Escalona. He completed his formal musical education studying harmony and composition with some of his grandfather's contemporaries and turned professional at the age of 15. Most of his experience as a bassist in Cuba was with Latin jazz and American music. As a professional, he worked with jazz musicians such as Nicolas Reynosa, Gonzalo Rubalcaba and Emiliano Salvador. Unlike his brother, drummer Samuel Formell, Juan-Carlos never played with Los Van Van.

During the daytime, Juan-Carlos attended school. Sent to live at the Isle of Pines from the age of 11 until he was 16, he worked five hours a day picking citrus fruit. It was very hard work for a small youngster. Most Americans don't understand that free education in Cuba carries with it hours and hours of manual labor to benefit the state. The children are not permitted to eat any of the fruit they pick; it is for export only. As a result, Cubans have become less and less familiar with their own produce. Formell believes that it is an abusive form of child labor, but at the same time it gave him the chance to meet real farm workers and find out about their lives. It gave him a strong love for the country and the natural beauty of Cuba, which has infused his music.

During his late teens, Formell developed a strong sense of spirituality. In 1990, when Formell was 26, Baha'i was featured at a world-wide Esperanto convention, and Formell and other Cubans began to practice Baha'i. At around the same time, Formell attended a small yoga class and learned meditation. This seemingly innocuous act was to have an unduly strong effect on his life. As Formell's reputation as a bassist grew, his career fell over a major stumbling block: he was not allowed to perform outside of Cuba. Even his father, by then the most popular musician inside Cuba, could not help him. It was just another instance of the workings of the Cuban government, which seems to formulate its decisions out of whimsy more than policy. Like Kafka's prisoner, Formell had to try to figure out why he was being singled out and what he had "done wrong." Formell decided that his problems with the government had to do with his yoga practice. Unlike Baha'i, yoga is essentially an individualistic practice. Since the practice of yoga is not a collective event, the government was unable to infiltrate, as it did with other religious practices. Yoga was thus the means to what the government considered a subversive act.

Juan-Carlos and his wife, Dita Sullivan, now live in an uptown New York City apartment. Ms. Sullivan is a writer and photographer who has lived in Cuba. The couple describe communism in Cuba as mind control. The government's messages bombard the people all the time. Even if they privately hated the government, they are obliged to attend public events and hear its messages. The government doesn't want their "inner radio" working in much the same way that it tries to keep foreign radio transmissions from reaching the Cuban people. To continue the metaphor, the government wants everyone in on the same wavelength. Individualism is the real enemy in a country where artistic expressions and religious practices are monitored and supervised.

Formell didn't feel at the time that he was doing something political with the quiet songs he began to write and perform. He wasn't saying, "Down with the government." He was just trying to stress what he felt, and what he knew other people felt. Nevertheless, stressing individuality is itself political in a situation where you're not allowed to be an individual.

Formell finally got the opportunity to travel abroad when the bassist scheduled to leave on a Mexican tour with the group Rumbavana died unexpectedly. Formell was permitted to fill in. Once he was in Mexico, he decided not to return to Cuba. Instead, he made his way slowly north to the border between the United States and Mexico, playing his guitar and singing in restaurants to make some money. When he got to the Rio Grande, he stripped and swam across with his clothing on his head. After being bailed out of an American jail by a family member, Formell went to New York and he began building an audience performing at the Zinc Bar. It was a difficult time for the young songwriter.

I came to New York as part of an exodus of young Cuban musicians who had no place in their country because the moment had been cut off. We came to New York looking for legends—the jazz club, the jam session, the all-night dances—but didn't find them. . . . There were restaurants and bars owned by Spanish-speaking people, but the music they wanted to hear was the sound of what used to be.[2]

In a nice twist of fate, Formell got his break when he was discovered by a Cuban, Juan de Marco González, a member of the Buena Vista Social Club. De Marco González recommended him to Nonesuch, and the word got out on the talented songwriter. Eventually Formell was signed to Wicklow Records (BMG Classics). His debut recording, *Songs from a Little Blue House* was nominated for a Grammy in the traditional tropical category. Also up for a Grammy in the salsa category was his father, who wound up winning the award for his album *Llego Los Van Van—Van Van Is Here* on Caliente Records.

While Juan-Carlos Formell's music has attracted an audience in the United States, people in this country have had difficulty placing him as an artist in the tradition of Cuban music. The reason is that his music is influenced by styles that are largely unfamiliar outside Cuba, or have fallen into disuse, such as *el feeling*. *El feeling* began in the 1940s with singer Olga Rivero. It is an outgrowth of the *bolero*, the ballad tradition of Cuban music. It is distinguished from earlier bolero songs by the sophisticated harmonies used to embellish American pop standards of the 1930s and 1940s. Unlike bolero, *el feeling* is typically sung with guitar accompaniment. José Antonio "Ñico" Rojas was one of the most famous *feeling* guitarists and an adventurous songwriter who delighted in delicate chromatic textures.[3] Other guitarist/songwriters were César Portillo de la Luz, author of *Contigo en la Distancia*, and José Antonio Méndez, author of *La Gloria Eres Tu*.

El feeling, like *bolero*, is music to listen to. It is not dance music per se, and the bass tends to play a purely harmonic role. In this respect, *el feeling* differs from Cuban genres that developed in city streets. In styles such as *el son*, the bass has a rhythmic role in addition to supplying the harmonic foundation. In many respects, the main difference between *el feeling* and *bolero* lies more in the way a song is interpreted than its other features. *Feeling* artists delivered a song in a dramatic manner, and "there was a tendency toward the recitative and the use of slides."[4] *Feeling* remains impossible to define. Perhaps songwriter Mario Fernández Porta put it best when he wrote: *El feeling* is a word that can't be explained, *el feeling* is a thing that comes from the heart."[5]

El feeling began to leave Cuba almost as soon as it was born. Olga Rivero and José Antonio Méndez both moved to Mexico in the late 1940s. During the next decade, Rivero retired, and Méndez remained there until he returned to Cuba in 1959. Both Felo Bohr and Reneé Barrios settled in Puerto Rico, and Pepe Reyes moved to Colombia and subsequently relocated to Argentina and Chile.[6]

Formell believes that *el feeling* also came to Brazil, where it influenced the development of bossa nova. The pioneers of bossa nova combined the traditional elements of Brazilian music with the harmonic element of *el feeling*. But for American musicians who are familiar with the sound of bossa nova and know nothing about *el feeling*, Formell sounds like a bossa nova guitarist. Formell disagrees. He is moving the old *feeling* guitar style forward, not copying bossa nova. It really has to do with his rhythmic approach, which is Cuban, not Brazilian. All of his music is in clave, which is the main difference between it and bossa nova.

El feeling disappeared after an international convention sponsored by Casa de las Américas called the "Meeting of the Protest Songs." After this event singers who came out of the *feeling* tradition turned to the folk-rock of the United States for inspiration, substituting the simple harmonies of this tradition for the advanced harmonies of *el feeling*. This new style was christened *nueva trova* and soon was given official support by the Cuban government. *Nueva trova* singers wrote songs protesting conditions in Argentina, Chile, or Nicaragua—never in Cuba. Formell does not consider it to be real Cuban music and dislikes its pretensions toward introversion and self-expression.

Formell is by no means an orthodox *feeling* artist like Omara Portuondo, the suave female vocalist in the Buena Vista Social Club.[7] In some of his songs, he takes a syncopated melody that is related to another Cuban style and gives it a *feeling* harmonic treatment. Moreover, *el feeling* is just one of the influences that make up Juan-Carlos Formell's music. Like his father, he has been inspired by changüi, the older cousin of *el son* from Guantánamo. In 1973, Los Van Van and Juan Formell recorded a version of the changüi classic *El Guararey de Pastora* (Formell called it *La Pastorita*).

While *el son* is in 4/4 time, changüi is an amalgam of 6/8 and 4/4, shifting almost imperceptibly between the two meters. Many of the same instruments are used in both *el son* and changüi: the bongos (larger in changüi, the maracas (smaller in changüi) and the tres guitar. Claves are found only in *el son*, and the güayo, a metal scraper, is only in changüi. In a *son* group there is a guitar in addition to the tres. The marimbula remains a fixture in changüi, while it was replaced by the string bass in *son* groups in the 1920s. *El son* is based on *son* clave, while rumba clave fits like a glove with the syncopated tres lines of changüi. It wasn't until recently that changüi has been introduced into the United States in a few recordings. The name had appeared stateside in several titles such as Arsenio Rodriguez's *Los Teenagers Bailan Changüi* and Celia Cruz's *Rico Changüi*, but these were not really in the changüi tradition.

Juan-Carlos Formell's recording *Songs from a Little Blue House* is a complex document and at times a bit difficult to decipher, but Formell's music is easy to listen to, and his originality is unmistakable. The music is dedicated to his grandmother María with the following note: "My white cloud comes back to her bed. The little blue house is the dearest memory. My song is born between sadness and yearning. Grandma María, rest in peace."[8] The cover of the CD is folded in such a way so that when pulled out of the pearl box it can be formed into a paper house, depicting the exterior and interior of the house in Oriente Province where María lived as a young girl, and which she delighted in describing to her grandson.

Songs from a Little Blue House begins in the sea with a dolphin song (*Canto Delfín*) that was written by the composer as an homage to the animal long thought of as a friend to people lost at sea. Then the recording goes on land for songs that are putatively about flowers, the siguaraya plant (a song composed by Lino Frías Hall), a crab, and a little bird. Most of Juan-Carlos Formell's songs are about the damage the Castro regime has wreaked on the island's culture. *Flores* is about someone hawking flowers: "Buy, buy my flowers." The song evolved from an experience Formell had when he was in Miami in 1995. During the evening he performed with another recent Cuban refugee, conguero Wicky Nogueras. In the daytime he accompanied Nogueras as he worked as a street vendor selling flowers. *Flores* concludes with words his grandmother spoke to him when he left Havana: "Child, be a pregonero so that the *son* will never die." A pregón is a song that street vendors sing to let people know they are selling their wares, and a pregonero is a street vendor. For many Cubans, the pregón contains the essence of Cuban culture. Actual pregónes and songs about vendors form a substantial part of the Cuban popular songbook. Some famous examples are *El Manicero* ("The Peanut Vendor"), and *Yerbero Moderno* ("The Modern Herb Vendor"). After the revolution, street vending was banned, and along with it the pregón songs disappeared. As a result, important aspects of Cuban culture died.

In the changüi-influenced song *El Pajarillo* Formell asks, Where is the little bird that used to sing about the coffee plantation and the loves of the country girl? A palm tree tells the singer that "The country folk have been robbed of their soul and their freedom." *Palo de Guayaba* ("Guava Stick") has the same theme: "guava stick, your freedom is at an end."

Formell concludes his CD with two songs that he juxtaposes most effectively. The first is *Mango Mangüe*, composed by Francisco "El Gran" Fellove, a showman who often performed with *filinistas (feeling* artists). The song has been recorded by Celia Cruz and other Cuban artists; there is also a 1948 Latin-jazz version by Charlie Parker. The second song, Formell's own, *A Cuba Nos Vamos* ("To Cuba We Go"), follows more or less the same melody as *Mango Mangüey*. In it, Formell states: "When the dictatorship ends I'm going to have a party. I'm going to dance and really celebrate, and if it doesn't end, this song will knock it down. It'll demolish it." He tells Fidel "we're finished with you," and he tells the Cuban people: "Don't give up. This day is coming."

Ten years ago the only places you could find Cuban records in New York City were the record store in Times Square and the Center for Cuban Studies. Now Cuban music is everywhere. This is not an accident. In a communist country where the arts are supervised by the government, it could not have happened without governmental support. The policy of opening up the Cuban music establishment to the free world has proven to be a great success. In an almost subliminal fashion it has persuaded people around the world that Cuba is not as bad as the Cuban exile community has made it out to be. And in a period when the Cuban government is encouraging the growth of the tourist industry, music has proven to be a potent advertisement for the charm of the island and its people.

The government has supported the export of timba, the modern Cuban sound, even though timba lyrics include some tepid criticisms of contemporary Cuban life. By allowing them onto the airways, the Cuban government appears to becoming less repressive than it really is. Besides, the government is aware that the lyrics are incomprehensible except to the people who are regular patrons of the outdoor dance venue el Tropical in Marianau, Havana, where the timba bands perform. Without translation, the information contained in these songs doesn't leave Cuba. The Cuban government itself doesn't understand what the words mean, and government workers have translated them incorrectly for foreign journalists. When the lyrics are understandable, they fail to address the real issues. Unlike reggae, for example, timba has no songs about repression or corruption.

Formell's voice is soft and cool, rather than hard and unyielding, as in the *sonero* tradition of Cuban singing that Americans are more accustomed to. Formell chooses to sing the way the Cuban people speak at home, especially about government repression: quietly. Some music reviewers have been unable to recognize that just because he doesn't shout doesn't mean his message isn't heard. According to Ms. Sullivan, it is very meaningful for Cubans that someone would sing these songs in *any* kind of voice.

11

Alfredo "Chocolate" Armenteros

Richard Davies

One of the most legendary debuts in the history of recorded music occurred when 21-year-old Alfredo "Chocolate" Armenteros played his trumpet solos on *Para las Niñas y para las Señoras* with Cuban bandleader René Alvarez in 1949. In Chocolate's case, this auspicious start was completely fulfilled in a career that is unmatched in the annals of Cuban brass playing. When Armenteros performed these aggressive solo spots on the Alvarez recording, he convincingly assumed his role as heir to the *septeto* trumpet tradition propagated by older masters such as Felix Chapotín and Enrique "Florecita" Velazco.

From his very first recordings, Armenteros has demonstrated a mature grasp of the Cuban style and a commanding technical prowess. In the five decades between *Para las Niñas y para las Señoras* and his still active New York City career, the septuagenarian has taken part in many of the landmark musical events in the historical development of the modern Afro-Cuban and salsa music styles. From the conjunto of Arsenio Rodríguez in the late 1940s to the bands of Eddie Palmieri and Larry Harlow in the 1960s heyday of salsa to the recent 1990s renaissance of descarga and other traditional Cuban styles instigated by Israel Cachao Lopez and others, Armenteros has been the most celebrated trumpet player in the history of modern Afro-Cuban/salsa music.

Alfredo "Chocolate" Armenteros was born on April 4, 1928, in Ranchuelo, Santa Clara, in the Cuban province of Las Villas. His mother was Angelina Abreu; his father, Lazaro Alfredo Armenteros, played trombone in his youth. Because of his early death, however, the elder Armenteros had little musical influence on the young Alfredo. In tribute, Armenteros displays his father's horn on his East Harlem apartment wall.

Among Armenteros' earliest listening experiences on the radio were recordings by the seminal *son* bands Sexteto Habanero and Septeto Nacional.[1] His first music teacher was Eduardo Egües (father of Richard Egües, the flute player for Orquesta Aragón). Eduardo Egües was a tenant of the Armenteros family and, in the process of creating a local children's musical group, he recruited Armenteros at the local public school. In the children's group, the training started with lessons in solfeggio and music theory. Only after a certain amount of proficiency was achieved in these areas would the student begin the study of an instrument. As fellow music students, Armenteros and Richard Egües were friends; Armenteros would often help Richard clean his father's "Academy," and they spent a good deal of the time practicing. As a result, Armenteros soon became a regular member of the children's band, where he improved his reading skills and was exposed to the brass literature. Armenteros's considerable performance skills are a testament to the highly regarded Cuban system of music education, which has produced generations of virtuoso musicians.

After moving to Havana in 1949, Armenteros began his professional career with the legendary Sexteto Habanero led by Gerardo Martínez, who was one of the original members. Habanero (along with Ignacio Pineiro's Septeto Nacional) was the most important early large *son* ensemble. Historically, Habanero traces its origins to the very earliest years of the twentieth century. Originally called the Trio Oriental, the group relocated from the eastern Oriente province (the cradle of the *son*) to Havana in 1910 and over the following decade gradually evolved into the Sexteto Habanero.[2] When Habanero and other early *son* groups added trumpet to increase the size of the group to seven pieces, the basic instrumentation (with some important later additions) and prototypical formal structures of the modern Afro-Cuban/salsa ensemble were set. The early septeto trumpet players (including the great Felix Chapotín) created the tradition that formed the core of the performance style of Armenteros and other mainstream modern-era Afro-Cuban/salsa brass players. Even though Armenteros's tenure with the past-their-heyday late 1940s version of Habanero was short-lived, an historical validation seems to have occurred when one of the most típico of modern Afro-Cuban trumpet players began his Havana career by working with the most tradition-laden Cuban *son* band.

Shortly afterward, Armenteros played on his first recordings with bandleader René Alvarez and his group Los Astros. Among these recordings was the aforementioned *Para las Niñas y para las Señoras*, which contains some of the most important early solo work by Armenteros. Even though he was just shy of his twenty-first birthday, Armenteros' solo style was fully developed. Andy González, noted New York bass player and salsa historian, considers the short trumpet solo sections on *Para las Niñas y para las Señoras* a textbook on Afro-Cuban style soloing: that if music students "study that solo, they will know what the 'swing' of *son* is."[3] Although the recording is difficult to find, its importance to Armenteros is signified by the position of a framed copy of the original 78 RPM recording on the wall of his apartment just below his father's trombone.

In addition to recording with Alvarez and Los Astros, Armenteros also performed in live performance with the group. It was during an engagement with Los Astros at the Polar Brewery in Havana that Arsenio Rodríguez, the most famous bandleader of the era, first heard the young trumpet player and offered him a job. Armenteros jumped at the chance of playing with Rodríguez and alongside the legendary trumpet maestro Felix Chapotín. For Armenteros, "working with Arsenio back then was the best; I felt like Amalia up in the seventh heaven didn't have it any better than me."[4] While his tenure with Rodríguez and his *conjunto* was not lengthy, Armenteros is represented on a number of the group's recordings.[5] The Rodríguez *conjunto* was the most celebrated ensemble of its type in the 1940s and was both a consolidation of the *son* tradition and a precursor to the New York City salsa movement that took place two decades later.

While the septeto instrumentation provided the core of the 1940s *conjunto*, there were a number of additions and alterations to the earlier *son* ensemble. As a tres player, Rodríguez continued to use this signal *son* instrument in his *conjunto*. The bass continued to be a part of the modern *conjunto*, but the *son* guitar was dropped and replaced by the piano. The bongo was the only hand drum used in the earlier *son* groups, and it was also used in the conjunto, albeit in a role that was more constrained and less freely improvisational than the earlier *son* bongo style. One of the most significant changes to the ensemble was the addition of the conga. Previously considered a crude unsophisticated street instrument and unsuitable for the indoor dancehall, this large hand drum added dramatically to the rhythmic drive of the modern conjunto.

Elements in trumpet performance also changed in the transition from the *son* septeto to the Rodríguez-style conjunto. The main change concerning the trumpet was the creation of a horn section with the addition of one or two other trumpeters to the single horn of the septeto. This development necessitated the creation of horn arrangements. There were two types of trumpet section arrangement used in the Arsenio Rodríguez conjunto. One type of arrangement was a setting of a typical septeto trumpet solo-like melody for the three trumpets of the conjunto using a mixture of unison and harmonized lines. This type of orchestration more closely reflected the *son* tradition than the alternative and more complex arranging style, which was influenced by the slick big band jazz scene of 1940s New York City. The famous Machito Afro-Cubans directed by Mario Bauzá and the Dizzy Gillespie jazz big band (which featured the Afro-Cuban compositions and conga playing of Chano Pozo) exemplified this second type of North American jazz-influenced arranging. The Arsenio Rodríguez conjunto utilized both types of arranging on their various recordings from the late 1940s when Armenteros performed with the band.

NO PUEDO COMER VISTAGACHA

An example of New York-style arranging is *No Puedo Comer Vistagacha*,[6] which was recorded in January 1950 and features impressive trumpet soloing by a 22-year-old Armenteros. Although this composition is closer to the New York style of arranging than other songs recorded by Rodríguez at the same time, this comparatively modern arrangement still reflects the *son* roots of the band as much as they emulate slicker New York influences (Machito et al.). *No Puedo Comer Vistagacha* contains excellent examples of the early Armenteros playing style. In order to provide a context for examining contemporary and later developments in the solo performance work of Armenteros, it is useful to examine this piece in some detail.

Structurally, *No Puedo Comer Vistagacha* is more complex than many of the Rodríguez compositions of the time. The *largo* section contains a relatively long form, and the *montuno* section is based on a four-measure pattern. This arrangement borrows modern New York-style elements in its brass orchestration.

An introduction of three bars leads into a *largo* section (Figure 1) that, although short in length, demonstrates the basic difference between a relatively complex *largo* and the repetitive short form of the *montuno*.

Figure 1. *Largo—No Puedo Comer Vistagacha.*

Instead of repeating a short harmonic pattern as in a *montuno* section, this *largo* uses a twelve-measure song form, starting with a two-measure melodic figure over the tonic harmony, which sequences in the third measure to start a whole step higher over the subdominant. The melody reaches the dominant harmony in the fifth measure of the form and is linearly contrasting while keeping the same rhythmic configuration. The dominant harmony extends over the next five measures, which include an extension of the last note of the figure in the fifth measure for two measures and a repetition of the fifth measure figure in measures 8 and 9. The harmony finally resolves in the eleventh measure of this section with a variation on the initial melodic module. The whole twelve-measure section is repeated, with brass replacing vocals during the first four bars.

The brass parts in the *largo* section use sophisticated jazz-like arranging techniques, similar to those employed at the time by the Machito band in New York City.[7] In *No Puedo Comer Vistagacha*, there are sophisticated ensemble trumpet parts supporting the vocalists when the trumpets are not in a leading role, which would rarely occur in a septeto-derived horn section arrangement. Besides using a variety of harmonic voicings, the three trumpets at times play a unison countermelody, most notably behind the vocal notes that are sustained in the sixth and seventh measures of the *largo* section. The final measure of the *largo* section's repetition uses a rhythmic break to lead into the *montuno* section of the piece.

The pattern of the *montuno* (and its associated *coro*) is based on a four-measure harmonic progression in B major (Figure 2).

Figure 2. *Coro/montuno* pattern—*No Puedo Comer Vistagacha*.

This section begins with a call-and-response (two alternations of *montuno* sections between the trumpet soloist and *coro*). The first of these two trumpet solos will be discussed below. The solo singer later replaces the trumpet for two more iterations of this call-and-response.

An intriguing variation of the typical practice for the *montuno* part is the expansion of the four-bar pattern to six measures during the *soneo*; the first four measures during the solo voice part are over a tonic pedal point and lead to a cadence in the fifth and sixth measures. A twelve-measure *tres* solo by Arsenio Rodríguez follows the final *coro*. The *tres* solo explains the choice of B major; it is a characteristic key for this stringed instrument. A six-measure ensemble break follows the twelve-measure solo.

The next part of the recording consists of a series of two-measure call-and-response sections. Built over a tonic pedal, these two-measure sections are performed alternately by the *coro* singing the title phrase "No puedo comer vistagacha" (which is adapted from the longer original *coro*) and either the trumpet section or a solo by Armenteros. The trumpet section responds to the *coro* in the first two instances. Armenteros begins soloing over the third iteration of the shortened *coro* and continues until the beginning of the fourth *coro*. The final iteration of the abbreviated *coro* is followed by the original four-measure *coro*, which serves as the ending phrase of the piece.

In his early solos with Rodríguez, Armenteros' instrumental virtuosity already surpassed the technique of older colleagues such as Chapotín and Velazco who recorded with the bandleader at the same time. Armenteros's fluid linear style contains a high percentage of sixteenth-note figures and shows the mastery of an impressive trumpet range. Armenteros's first solo in *No Puedo Comer Vistagacha* includes a high concert C#6 and his lines display a rhythmic subtlety that defies notational representation and belies the youth of the 22 year old (Figure 3).

Figure 3. First trumpet solo—*No Puedo Comer Vistagacha.*

Armenteros precedes the *montuno* pattern of his first solo with a three eighth-note pickup figure, and the final part of this solo extends into the first two beats of the following *coro* section. This short solo is a masterpiece in the Afro-Cuban art of stretching and compressing a melodic line over the underlying rhythm. Andy González compares this effect to the stretching and releasing of a rubber band.[8] While the three pickup notes coincide with the underlying eighth-note rhythms, the following measure stretches the eighth notes of the figures almost into quarter-note triplets. In the last beat-and-a-half of the second measure of the *montuno* pattern, six ascending sixteenth notes reestablish the melodic line to the center part of the pulse. This return to rhythmic equilibrium is disturbed immediately a beat later when the first of four one-and-a-half-beat motives again stretches behind the rhythmic underpinning. Each of these motives consists of four sixteenth notes and an eighth rest. Following the time stretch of the first motive, the time compresses gradually during the succeeding three motives until, by the second beat of the fourth bar of the *montuno* pattern, Armenteros is playing on the front part of the beat. Finally, Armenteros introduces the next *coro* with yet another delaying action on the final three notes of this solo. This short trumpet solo demonstrates an incredible mastery of both trumpet technique and rhythmic manipulation, which is even more impressive when the youthful age of this trumpet prodigy is considered.

THE 1950s

In the early 1950s, Armenteros played with various groups, including the famous Sonora Mantancera. While on tour in Mexico with the group in 1951, Armenteros met Machito, singer and bandleader of one of the most famous Latin groups on the New York scene in the 1940s and 1950s. Machito offered Armenteros a job in his New York-based orchestra. However, Armenteros was planning a musical collaboration with his cousin Beny Moré, and that collaboration was in the planning stages. While flattered by the job offer from Machito, Armenteros decided to remain in Cuba and participate in the inception of his cousin's band. Moré is considered by many to be the greatest singer in Afro-Cuban music history. His large band became the toast of Havana in the mid-1950s in much the same way that Machito (along with Tito Puente and Tito Rodríguez) ruled the New York mambo scene. Many of the Beny Moré recordings on which Armenteros performed in the mid-1950s have been reissued on CD, including the release *Yo Hoy Como Ayer* by Beny Moré y su Orquesta Gigante de Estrellas Cubana.[9] Unfortunately, there are no Armenteros solos on these recordings. Much of this material consists of big band instrumentation with set arrangements and very little spontaneous instrumental soloing.

Armenteros played with Moré's band from 1953 to 1956. In addition, throughout the 1950s, he was a busy Havana studio musician and a staff member of the studio orchestra of the Cuban radio and television station CMQ.[10] Besides working with Moré, Armenteros performed and/or recorded with numerous other musicians and groups in Cuba in the 1950s before his relocation to New York.[11] During this time, he recorded with the famed Latin jazz bandleader/composer Chico O'Farrill, who was closely associated with Dizzy Gillespie. Another well-known musician Armenteros recorded with in the late 1950s was pianist Bebo Valdés, who is now best known as the father of piano virtuoso Chucho Valdés. One of the trumpeter's most renowned Havana record dates in the 1950s was *Cole Español*, featuring the American pop singer Nat "King" Cole. Other Cuban artists Armenteros performed with before his move north were singers Cheo Marquetti and Joseito Fernández. The latter composed the Cuban standard *Guantanamera*, which was recorded by Armenteros over two decades later on *Chocolate y Amigos*.

Armenteros made his initial foray to New York City in the late 1950s on tour with flute player José Fajardo. In 1960, he relocated permanently to New York and finally joined the Machito band, starting a long on-and-off relationship with the orchestra, which has survived to this day with Machito's son taking the reins as bandleader following his father's death. Armenteros insists that the politics of Castro's revolution had very little to do with his decision to immigrate to New York. Armenteros asserts that "I have never been involved in politics. I've been a musician all my life and that's it."[12] His reason for relocating was to accept the longstanding offer by Machito and Mario Bauzá to join the Machito orchestra. Because Armenteros had recently left his cousin Beny Moré's group, the trumpeter readily accepted this new offer of employment.

Besides working with Fajardo and Machito in New York, Armenteros quickly became busy as a freelance trumpet player, recording with almost every up-and-coming New York *salsa* bandleader. In the 1960s and 1970s, Armenteros worked with Eddie Palmieri, Charlie Palmieri, Larry Harlow, Johnny Pacheco, Mongo Santamaría, Ismael Rivera and Roberto Torres. One early (1964) salsa record album he played on was Orlando Marín's *Que Chevere, Volume II.* Armenteros also performed on many recordings released by the major Latin labels and performed by their studio "All-Star" groups such as the Tico All-Stars, Alegre All-Stars, and Fania All-Stars.[13] His recording work with pianist/bandleader Eddie Palmieri is of particular importance and will be examined in more detail.

SALSA

The term *salsa* was coined in the late 1960s and early 1970s and is generally attributed to the publicity efforts of certain Latin music industry executives.[14] Regardless of its origins, salsa has come to represent to many the whole of Afro-Cuban music. For the purposes of this discussion, salsa will be defined in two different ways. In addition to its universal meaning, the term salsa also refers more specifically to music from the New York Latin scene that developed during the 1960s and 1970s. This narrower usage refers to the music of artists like Charlie and Eddie Palmieri, Larry Harlow, Willie Colón, Johnny Pacheco and others who recorded for labels such as Alegre, Tico and Fania starting in the early 1960s. In most cases, this more limited definition of salsa will be assumed although the phrase "salsa song" will on occasion be used to refer to any type of song in the *son* tradition.

The New York salsa scene of the 1960s and 1970s is of paramount importance to the examination of the Armenteros solo performance style. When he made his landmark recordings with Eddie Palmieri (e.g., *Justicia* and *Superimposition*), Armenteros was in his early forties and at the peak of his instrumental prowess. In his extended solos on these recordings, he was able to push the envelope of the típico Cuban solo trumpet style well beyond its conservative role in the earlier (1940s) mainstream *conjunto*. His work with Palmieri and on other recordings of 1970s such as the two volumes released by the Grupo Folklórico y Experimental Nuevayorquino represents one of the high-water marks of Armenteros' career and some of the most notable recorded trumpet solo playing in the Afro-Cuban/salsa historical continuum.

A number of influences factored into the development of salsa. The most important influence was the Cuban *son* and *conjunto* tradition as represented by groups such as Sexteto Habanero and the *conjunto* of Arsenio Rodríguez. It can be convincingly argued that salsa is simply a renaming and updating of the *son conjunto* genre. Although this assertion is in many ways valid, several other factors (both musical and nonmusical) contributed to the particular manner in which salsa music evolved. In addition to the *son conjunto* (and to an important extent the traditional charanga), the other primary musical influences on salsa were the Latin jazz bands of New York from the 1940s (such as those led by Dizzy Gillespie and Machito), the large Cuban bands of the 1950s (like the one led by singing star Beny Moré), and the mambo movement centering around New York clubs (most notably the Palladium) that reached its zenith in the 1950s via the bands led by the big three: Tito Puente, Tito Rodríguez and Machito.[15] Yet another significant influence on salsa is the descarga, or Cuban jam session, which originated in Cuba in the mid-1950s and is most closely associated with the bassist Israel Cachao Lopez.

Although North American music of the time had stylistic effects on salsa (most notably in the *búgalu*), its main influence showed up in the economically induced reduction in ensemble size. Ironically, the trend toward smaller groups in the Latin field actually created a renaissance of traditional Cuban forms in most of the early salsa bands as the reduction in size created ensembles that more closely resembled the instrumentation of the earlier Cuban *conjuntos* and charangas than of the 1950s New York Latin big band. One of the first events to involve the new generation of New York salsa musicians was the charanga craze of the early 1960s. Duboney, the charanga group led by pianist Charlie Palmieri (and featuring flutist Johnny Pacheco) is generally credited with being the initial force in creating the new musical fashion.[16] The band that Charlie Palmieri formed, with its four violins and flute, was a distinct departure from the brass- and saxophone-dominated music of the previous two decades.

In addition to the flute/violin front line, there were other instrumental changes that resulted from the charanga vogue of the early 1960s. The percussion instrument most closely associated with the traditional danzón and charanga was the timbal. This instrument reasserted its dominance in the rhythm section during this charanga revival and continued to be included as well in most of the New York horn section-driven *conjuntos* that took over the salsa scene following the brief charanga craze. Additionally, there was a duet-based singing style and "a classicism of sound and form that gave the charangas a grace and tension quite new to the New York scene."[17]

By the mid-1960s, the popularity of the charanga waned, and the instrumentation of most of the mainstream salsa bands switched from the charanga instrumentation to that of the *conjunto*. Perhaps the most famous example is Johnny Pacheco, who switched to the *conjunto* format when he started Fania Records in 1964.[18] A musical conservative, Pacheco emulated the traditional *conjunto* to the point of recording several covers (or remakes) of Arsenio Rodríguez compositions. Progressive salsa bandleaders like Larry Harlow and Eddie Palmieri also covered Rodríguez compositions.

While the *conjunto* became the most dominant format for salsa ensembles, most of these bands retained some aspects of the charanga instrumentation. The classic *conjunto* of the 1940s did not use the timbales; the new salsa bands added this instrument (and its mounted cowbells) to create, along with the congas and bongos, a three-man drum battery. The late timbalero Tito Puente had anticipated this move in his band years earlier. Because Pacheco played the flute, he included this charanga instrument in his otherwise traditional trumpet-oriented *conjunto*.

Another band that included both the flute and timbales in a *conjunto* format was the innovative La Perfecta, led by Eddie Palmieri (Charlie's younger brother). Eddie Palmieri's band was considered by many to be the seminal group of the early salsa era.[19] One major innovation of this group was the use of trombones in place of trumpets. This change came about through the collaboration of Palmieri and trombonist Barry Rogers. Because of the band's use of trombones alongside the charanga-associated flute and timbales, Palmieri's brother Charlie coined the term trombanga to describe La Perfecta. The use of trombones instead of trumpets as the horn section was an innovation by La Perfecta that had a major influence on salsa bands in the mid-1960s, such as the one led by salsa legend Willie Colón.

A new instrumentation change that became common in the late 1960s and early 1970s was an increase in the size of the horn section. Although many groups still utilized the all-trumpet or all-trombone horn formation, a number of salsa bands began to use a larger brass configuration: combining two trumpets with two trombones and creating a powerful and versatile horn section, made even more formidable, in many cases, by the addition of a baritone saxophone on the bottom. Many of the groups associated with Fania Records used this extended horn section format and this format was often used on recordings led by Armenteros in later years. Variations of this particular five-piece horn section combination are still commonplace on the current salsa scene.

One of the first salsa groups to record using a four-piece horn section with two trumpets and two trombones was Orchestra Harlow, led by pianist Larry Harlow. In the years immediately preceding his first work with Eddie Palmieri, Armenteros recorded a number of albums with Orchestra Harlow on the Fania label. Two of these albums were *Gettin' Off (Bajandote)* (released in 1967) and *Heavy Smokin'*, which followed a year later. Although he was featured sporadically on all these albums, his soloing skills are prominently demonstrated on *Heavy Smokin'*. His solo playing on *Heavy Smokin'* holds added significance in that it precedes his classic work with Eddie Palmieri.

On *La Juventud*, he performs a solo in a setting that recalls the mainstream 1940s *conjunto* style. Although the solo is relatively short in length and is placed over the ongoing *coro*, its facile technical maturity and highly charged rhythmic drive anticipate the classic 1970s Armenteros performances with Palmieri and Grupo Folklórico. On *Chez José*, in response to four-bar *coros* over a minor key *montuno*, he plays a series of solo spots, which are pensive yet show off his impressive technical skills. Armenteros's work here demonstrates his finely tuned Cuban-style rhythmic sensibilities.

On *Rica Combinación*, Armenteros's soloing over the two cowbell-driven salsa swing is a miniature version of his playing on future Palmieri classics like *Justicia, Se Acabó*, and *Bilongo*. His Cuban roots shine through in a couple of short solo spots on the dancehall rumba *Mi Guaguancó*. In the septeto tradition, *María La O* starts with an introductory horn section statement of the solo vocalists' *largo* melody. After the *largo*, the trombonists perform the instrumental version of the *coro* figure with Armenteros providing improvised trumpet responses. Before the vocal *coro* and soneo take over, there are four iterations of the trombone section/trumpet solo version (the final one overlapping with the singers). Following a bongo solo and a horn section riff figure, Armenteros plays an extended solo over the *coro*. The brief return of the soneo and a final brass break bring the piece to a conclusion.

THE DESCARGA

A major influence on Cuban-derived music's evolution in the salsa era was the descarga. Most closely associated with the bassist Israel Cachao Lopez, the descarga is a Cuban jam session. Because the descarga started in Cuba, it is relatively free of jazz influences. Whereas the Latin jazz that evolved in the 1940s and 1950s around musicians like Machito and Dizzy Gillespie was highly influenced by the language of modern jazz, the descarga was purely Cuban in origin. Instead of applying the exotic harmony and virtuosic lines of modern jazz to the clave context (in the manner of Dizzy Gillespie and others), the descargas that Cachao began recording in the late 1950s were firmly anchored in the Afro-Cuban tradition.

Although descargas sometimes include vocals, in most cases they are instrumental pieces based on simple *montuno* patterns. However, instead of being limited to the call-and-response role prescribed in the septetos and *conjuntos*, the horn players in a descarga stretch out and perform longer solos. Often, one horn player plays a continuous figure while another performer improvised. This practice of riffing behind a soloist had a strong influence on salsa bands such as the one led by Eddie Palmieri. This riff figure was referred to as a *moña*. Cachao's descarga group, like the salsa *conjunto*, also utilized the three-piece percussion combo of bongo, conga and timbales.

The descarga format was borrowed and given a New York flavor when Charlie Palmieri led a series of recorded jam sessions in the mid-1960s for Al Santiago's record company Alegre.[20] Alegre (along with Tico Records) was one of the most prominent early salsa labels. The "label band," Alegre All-Stars, recorded several albums structured along the same line as the earlier Cuban descarga. Although there were more jazz elements present in this new descarga than in its Cuban cousin, the standard forms of the *son conjunto* were utilized in much the same way that artists like Cachao borrowed the traditional Cuban genres in their mid-1950s Havana-based descarga. The Alegre All-Stars existed for a short time and produced only a handful of recordings, yet their influence was extensive; there were numerous copycat studio bands, including the Tico All-Stars and the Fania All-Stars that represented the other major record labels of the salsa era.[21] Although Armenteros participated in some of the early descarga recordings, his most noted work in this format came later. These include the instrumentals on Eddie Palmieri's *Superimposition* album from the early 1970s and the revival recordings that Israel Cachao López produced in the 1990s, which include *Master Sessions, Volumes I and II* and the Andy Garcia-produced movie *Como Su Ritmo No Hay Dos*.

EDDIE PALMIERI

When the original La Perfecta disbanded in the late 1960s, Eddie Palmieri continued to record and perform with variations of the original band. One change was the replacement of the flute by a trumpet. On most of the Palmieri recordings at this time, Armenteros was the featured trumpet soloist. Some of the best solo playing in Armenteros's career is represented on the classic Palmieri recordings *Justicia* and *Superimposition*. These two volumes contain several examples of the mature Armenteros solo style. His work on *Bilongo* from *Superimposition* is one of the most renowned examples of trumpet soloing in the history of Afro-Cuban/salsa music.

There are three primary types of composition on which Armenteros is featured on these two albums. One is the remake of a song originally recorded by earlier Afro-Cuban ensembles such as the early *son* groups from the 1920s and 1930s or the *conjuntos* from the 1940s. In homage to the Afro-Cuban tradition, these pieces are performed in a more conservative manner than the other selections on these albums. *Lindo Yambú* on *Justicia* and *Pa' Huele* on *Superimposition* are examples of this type of piece. Another type of composition is the instrumental descarga, which is represented on *Superimposition* by *17.1* and *Chocolate Ice Cream*. Armenteros is listed as composer on *Chocolate Ice Cream*, but (like *17.1*) it is basically a studio jam session.

The third type of composition is the up-tempo mainstream salsa original. *Se Acabó* from *Superimposition* and the title tune on *Justicia* are examples. Although *Bilongo* is an older standard song, it is also treated in much the same manner as these two songs. After briefly discussing examples of each of these three composition types, Armenteros's work on *Bilongo* will be examined in some detail.

The two remakes, *Lindo Yambú* and *Pa' Huele*, are tributes to the Cuban *son* tradition. Ignacio Piñeiro and Septeto Nacional originally recorded *Lindo Yambú* in 1930. The Palmieri version is very different than the Piñeiro recording and is closer in conception to a 1940s modern *conjunto* approach as exemplified by Arsenio Rodríguez. *Pa' Huele*, on the other hand, is very similar in many ways to its Rodríguez-originated prototype. Both pieces contain newer musical elements that were introduced by New York salsa musicians as well as traditional Cuban elements. The time honored Cuban call-and-response tradition is held in highest regard on these two pieces. Because of the stylistic authenticity that Armenteros brought to the Palmieri setting, it seems appropriate that the trumpeter's first recording with the pianist was *Lindo Yambú*. On both this tune and on *Pa' Huele*, Armenteros is conservative in his approach. While his work here is more expansive than it would have been in the earlier *conjunto* period, it is much less freewheeling and extended than his playing on the other selections of these Palmieri albums. In the typical *son* manner, Armenteros plays two solo responses to the four-measure *coro* on *Lindo Yambú* before being replaced by the solo singer. Also, as in a typical Rodríguez *conjunto* piece (albeit in a broader manner), the Armenteros trumpet rides over the top of the entire ensemble at various times throughout the recording.

While it has a much simpler formal structure than *Lindo Yambú*, *Pa' Huele* has more extensive trumpet soloing than the Piñeiro remake. In this case, the entire piece (like the Rodríguez version) is a *montuno* from beginning to end. The piece opens with a Palmieri piano emulation of the Rodríguez tres figure on the original recording with the rest of the rhythm section entering four measures later. This is followed by a repeating four-bar *coro* figure, the first two iterations of which alternate with unison (octave) brass figures similar melodically to a typical septeto trumpet line. Following the third *moña*, the sonero replaces the brass section in the call-and-response patterns with the *coro*. At this point a two-cowbell figure is introduced that identifies this recording as unmistakably New York salsa in origin. Although Afro-Cuban music prior to the salsa period made use of cowbell, the combination of the bongocero and timbalero switching at the same time to similar cowbell patterns is a trademark of New York salsa. After a piano solo and break, the horn section plays a repeated eight-measure figure over a shortened *coro*. This *coro* is continued while Armenteros plays an aggressive solo that (although comparatively short in duration) is more reflective of the new salsa mode of soloing than the playing by Chapotín and others in the Rodríguez era. As the short *coro* continues, the soneo returns and is again replaced with the *coro*, which in turn is replaced by a series of *moñas* with an overlay of trumpet soloing much in the *son conjunto* tradition of ending a piece. In this case, the soneo returns once more before the recording ends with horn-section figures.

The descarga selections on *Superimposition (Chocolate Ice Cream* and *17.1)* feature some of the longest trumpet solos by Armenteros at the time. *Chocolate Ice Cream* utilizes a number of elements derived from North American music such as pentatonic and blues scales that are used to perfection by Palmieri on his piano solo. While Armenteros lacks the finesse of the leader in his use of these foreign (to the Afro-Cuban style) musical devices, the trumpeter's technical skills and buoyant self-assurance carry the day. Like *17.1, Chocolate Ice Cream* is uncharacteristic in that the trumpet solo is performed sans *moña* figures for an extended period of time.

17.1 is performed at a brighter tempo than *Chocolate Ice Cream* and contains the simplest harmonic material: a continuous unresolved dominant seventh chord. After Palmieri's piano solo, a timbale solo by Nicky Marrero intensifies the rhythmic thrust. Armenteros adds to the drive on his solo. Although this solo also starts out unaccompanied before the trombone *moña* appears, it is for a much shorter period of time than on *Chocolate Ice Cream*.

It is on the original *son conjunto* style compositions of *Justicia* and *Superimposition* that the solo playing of Armenteros is expressed most fully. *Se Acabó* and *Bilongo* from *Superimposition* and the title tune from *Justicia* are the selections most representative of the hard-core Palmieri salsa style and contain the most extended, adventurous and vibrant soloing by Armenteros to that point. All three of these selections have relatively complex *largo* structures. The horn section arrangements vary from elaborate orchestrations as in *Justicia* to the extemporaneous background trumpet improvisations of *Bilongo*. *Justicia* and *Bilongo* both contain piano solos, and *Justicia* and *Se Acabó* have percussion solos over a highly charged cowbell-driven rhythm section. One role of these various solos is to set up lengthy *moña*-backed trumpet solo sections, which are typically over 80 measures in length. The extremely syncopated trombone *moñas* add even more momentum to the already undulating rhythmic underpinnings. On *Justicia* and *Se Acabó*, the continuously evolving two-trombone *moñas* are performed using both harmonized lines and contrapuntal textures. A single trombonist (José Rodrigues) performs the *moñas* behind Armenteros on *Bilongo*. In all three recordings, the initial *moña* figures precede the start of the trumpet solo. All these trumpet solos feature a rich mixture of virtuoso lines, syncopated rhythmic figures and bravura high notes. *Bilongo* is the most celebrated of these three solos and will be analyzed in more detail.

BILONGO

The standard song *Bilongo* has been recorded many times since it was published in 1957. Singer Tito Rodríguez and his popular 1950s band produced one of the first and most renowned recordings of the Guillermo Rodríguez Fiffe composition. Since then there have been numerous recordings of the song, including the Eddie Palmieri version on *Superimposition*. One reason for the popularity of this song is its unique *largo* structure. The *largo* starts in two-three clave and reverses clave four times using odd-numbered phrase lengths before a final reversal back to two-three as the *montuno* section and *coro* begin.

From beginning to end, the Palmieri recording is an unrelenting performance, featuring some of the most renowned trumpet soloing in the history of Afro-Cuban/salsa music. Palmieri and the rhythm section start the recording with a G minor vamp, which after four measures is joined by a soloing Armenteros for eight additional measures. Numerous trumpet players have memorized this famous trumpet introduction during the past 25 years. Throughout most of the 56 measure *largo*, Armenteros provides continuous virtuoso mellismatic figures behind singer Ismael Quintana's rendition of the melody.

The *montuno* section begins with a series of *coro*/sonero call-and-responses and a brief piano solo. A repeated piano vamp introduces the *montuno*/solo section. Trombonist José Rodrigues plays a series of extended *moña* figures over which Armenteros solos for more than 80 measures. In order to examine the mature Armenteros style, two examples from this tour-de-force trumpet solo will be more closely analyzed.

Figure 4 starts on measure 181 of the recording and has many characteristics of the *septeto* trumpet tradition.

Figure 4. First solo excerpt—Bilongo.

Following the two eighth-note octave leap on the first beat of measure 181, a series of three-beat figures sets up an implied ¾ meter against the underlying 4/4 clave. This is a common occurrence in Afro-Cuban trumpet playing and happens a number of times in this solo, often in a more direct manner. Measures 182 and 183 demonstrate another typical feature of Afro-Cuban music: the use of the descending melodic minor scale over the dominant harmony. Armenteros often makes these substitutions when he solos in a minor key. A related feature (typical of Cuban soloing) is the substitution of the seventh chord built over the minor seventh degree of the scale (in this case F7) for the dominant harmony (D7). In measure 182 and the first half of measure 183, Armenteros continuously arpeggiates through an F7 chord.

Another example of the use of the descending melodic minor scale is the four-and-a-half bars of the solo represented in Figure 5.

Figure 5. Second solo excerpt—*Bilongo*.

Most of the phrase starting on the second beat of measure 197 is composed of a highly embellished descending G minor scale. An impressive example of trumpet technique, the ornamented line moves almost two octaves from the C above the staff to the D below the staff (and a lower neighbor note C#) twelve beats later. Using a series of lower neighbor tones and eighth-note triplets, Armenteros plays the descending line with an impressive virtuosity. Although this line utilizes both the ascending and descending melodic minor scale versions of the sixth and seventh scale degrees, the ascending versions (E and F#) are used almost exclusively as neighbor notes and leading tones to a returning scale degree. When the notes are part of the main line, the descending versions (Eb and F) are always used. The tension of this long and rhythmically dense descending motion is relieved in the last four beats of the phrase with an ascending diatonic arpeggio. Although these two four-measure figures are only a minute part of Armenteros's classic work on *Bilongo*, they demonstrate important aspects of his solo style in the early 1970s.

GRUPO FOLKLÓRICO Y EXPERIMENTAL NUEVAYORQUINO

In 1975, two events played an important role in Armenteros's career. One was the release of a two-volume recording by a workshop group of musicians, organized by musicologist René López, with the daunting name Grupo Folklórico y Experimental Nuevayorquino. The other significant event for Armenteros was the start of his career as a leader with the recording *Chocolate Aquí*.

Grupo Folklórico was a renaissance movement featuring some of the best young New York musicians of the mid-1970s as well as Cuban veterans like Armenteros. Most of the musicians involved in the project were mainstream New York City-based salsa musicians. However, the organizing element behind the recording was the return to Afro-Cuban (and Afro-Puerto Rican) fundamentals. By reconsidering fundamental Cuban elements like the rumba and the *son*, the music was revitalized. The group was a mixture of young (mostly Puerto Rican) musicians like the González brothers (Jerry and Andy) who were dogged in their pursuit of historical knowledge about the Cuban style, and older musicians like Armenteros who were a product of that tradition. Armenteros is prominently featured in several selections on the two volumes. His trumpet playing was an essential element in this tribute to traditional Afro-Cuban music in its myriad manifestations.

Although both volumes of the recording contain important pieces, we will examine the first volume in more detail. *Cuba Linda* begins with a lengthy conga solo, which evolves into a series of drum section breaks and finally into a traditional dancehall guaguancó. Armenteros plays a brief introductory solo over the initial tonic pedal before a sixteen-measure chant melody and chord progression are performed twice in the rumba tradition of substituting syllabic sounds for words. A short trumpet solo interlude leads to the solo singer and the extended main portion of the *largo* form. Armenteros supports the sonero through much of this section with background soloing. When the *coro* and *montuno* section finally arrive after an extensive prolongation of the *largo*, the three-two rumba clave and the usual call-and-response between *coro* and sonero are established. After several repetitions, Armenteros replaces the solo singer and plays his longest solo on the piece over the ongoing *coro*. Following piano, flute and percussion solos, the *coro* and overlapping horn *moñas* bring the piece to its final coda section.

Armenteros is credited as the composer of *Chocolate's Guajira*, which is a typical slow tempo minor key *guajira*. The *guajira* is a musical form that Armenteros has returned to continually throughout his career. His initial soloing, both in the introduction and in the following call-and-response section, is moody and less technical than his playing on the earlier Palmieri sides. After a lengthy sonero and solos by the tres and flute, a fairly lengthy vocal speaking dialogue ensues between the singer and Armenteros over the ongoing *coro*. Trombone and flute enter with contrapuntal *moñas* at the end of the dialogue section and introduce an overriding trumpet solo. Although the trumpet playing is more complex and virtuosic at this point than at the beginning of the piece, it is still very conservative and *típico*.

Anabacoa is a guaguancó based on a two-measure *montuno* pattern that is unchanging throughout the entire piece. The trombone, trumpet and flute alternate improvised solos with the *coro* for two sequences. These two four-bar solo spots are the total extent of Armenteros' improvised work on this selection. *Adelaida* and *Luz Delia* are both examples of traditional folk styles associated primarily with Puerto Rico. Although interesting in their own right, neither selection contains soloing by Armenteros. On *Carmen La Ronca*, the trumpeter begins the piece *son* style by playing the first part of the vocal melody. When the solo singer enters with the same melody, Armenteros plays background figures throughout the vocal *largo*. After the recapitulation of the *largo* (with trumpet introduction), Armenteros trades *montunos* with the *coro*. After four solos, the trumpet is replaced by the sonero. These four solos are examples of the mature Armenteros in complete command of his medium. The *coro*/sonero section leads to a tres solo followed by a conga solo. Armenteros then plays a lengthy solo, which is similar in style to his playing on the earlier Palmieri recordings. The solo begins and ends with the trumpeter intoning the *coro* melody. After a few *coro* and sonero trades, the piece ends with a single horn section performance of the *coro* melody.

After two Santeria-influenced and batá-driven pieces that consist almost entirely of percussion and vocals (albeit the second one contains fine playing by bassist Andy González), Armenteros is featured again on *A Papá y Mamá*. *A Papá y Mamá* is a freewheeling dancehall rumba featuring an abundance of traditional chants and some of the most exciting playing by Armenteros on the entire volume. His opening phrases over the initial tonic pedal are somewhat reminiscent of his famous introduction on Eddie Palmieri's *Bilongo* a few years earlier. Armenteros provides sporadic fill figures throughout the lengthy *largo* section, which consists of numerous exchanges between wordless vocal chants and lyric-based sections. The numerous exchanges between *coro* and trumpet solo at the beginning of the *montuno* section demonstrate Armenteros's mastery of the primordial *son*-based call-and-response trumpet solo style.

Volume Two of the Grupo Folklórico recording features another diverse set of compositions. In addition to the mixture of traditional Cuban and Puerto Rican forms, there is also a Brazilian number, *Ao Meu Lugar Voltar*, which features a Brazilian singer. Armenteros is featured on four numbers. The album opens with *Cinco En Uno Calletero*, which features the trumpet player at various places throughout. The guaguancó *Trompeta en Cueros* is a tour de force for Armenteros and was reprised a decade later on the Armenteros recording *Chocolate en Sexteto*. This selection contains some of his best soloing on the entire two-album recording. *La Mamá* is an old guaguancó that in this case contains Santería elements in the use of a battery of traditional batá drums. Armenteros and trombonist José Rodrigues both provide notable solos on this piece. *Dime La Verdad* is a bolero-*son* in the old septeto style. The trumpeter's *típico* soloing is compared to the master Florecita (one of Armenteros's mentors) in the notes accompanying the recording.

CHOCOLATE: THE LEADER

An impressive body of work is represented on the numerous recordings Armenteros produced as a leader during the 1970s and 1980s, a period that represents his peak years as a trumpet soloist. Except for Armenteros's very first recording as a leader, *Chocolate Aqui* (released in 1975 by the Carib Música label), these recordings can be divided into three basic groupings, each of which can be identified by the particular label he was signed with at the time. Each grouping will be identified by the label name. Chronologically, the three labels are Salsoul, SAR and Caiman.

Three of Armenteros's albums from the mid-1970s were eventually consolidated on the Salsoul label and can be considered as one grouping. *Chocolate Caliente* and *Juntos* (a collaboration with Roberto Torres) were originally released on the Mericana label and later reissued on Salsoul. *Chocolate en el Rincon* was released in 1976 directly on Salsoul. The second grouping of recordings includes the three albums *Prefiero El Son, Y Sigo Con Mi Son* and *Chocolate Dice*, all of which were released on the SAR label in the early 1980s. The first two have been re-released in CD form as *Lo Mejor de Chocolate, Volumes 1 and 2*. These three SAR recordings were the most *típico* that he had recorded up to this time. The Caiman albums, the last of the three groupings, were recorded in the mid-1980s and contain Armenteros' most descarga and Latin jazz-oriented recordings as a leader. Using an all-instrumental format with Mario Rivera sharing the front line on baritone saxophone, Armenteros exhibits his most extended soloing as a leader on the Caiman recordings: *Chocolate en Sexteto, ¡Rompiendo Hielo!* and *Chocolate y Amigos*.

CHOCOLATE AQUI

Coinciding chronologically with the Grupo Folkórico recordings was the release of the first recording to feature Armenteros as a leader: *Chocolate Aqui*. This album, released in 1975 on the Carib Musica label and featuring rhythm section, singers and the solo horn of Armenteros, is more reflective of the "back to the roots" values that surfaced in the Grupo Folklórico recordings than of the modernistic salsa associated with the post-La Perfecta recordings by Eddie Palmieri that featured extended solos by Armenteros. Most of the 10 selections on the album are firmly in the Afro-Cuban tradition but without the primal energy of the Grupo Folklórico recordings. One area in which *Chocolate Aqui* differs from a typical *conjunto* recording is the extended role of the trumpet soloist. Although there are vocals on the album, they are mostly in the form of *coros*. There are a number of examples of solo singing, but they are primarily limited in use to *largo* sections and an occasional sonero in a *montuno* section. In most of the tunes, the trumpet replaces the solo singer in call-and-response exchanges with the *coro*.

SALSOUL

In 1975 Armenteros released the first of his three albums on the Salsoul label. Entitled *Chocolate Caliente*, the album features a larger and more dynamic instrumentation than *Chocolate Aqui*. Although considered by many to be superior to the earlier recording because of its higher production values and energy level, *Chocolate Caliente* nevertheless lacks some of the lyrical intimacy of Armenteros's playing on *Chocolate Aqui*. In January 1977, Salsoul released *Chocolate En El Rincon*, which features Manny Oquendo and Andy González (both of whom later turned the Grupo Folklórico project into the internationally acclaimed Conjunto Libre). The final Salsoul release is a collaboration between Armenteros and producer Roberto Torres entitled *Juntos* (although it was originally recorded in 1974). All three Salsoul albums are similar in concept and personnel.

Armenteros shares leader billing with Roberto Torres on *Juntos*. This collaboration is important in that Torres later produced the Armenteros recordings on the SAR label, which was headed by Torres. Although released later, *Juntos* was actually recorded in 1974 and predates *Chocolate Aqui*. With 10 selections, *Juntos* is a slicker production than the other two Salsoul recordings and contains intricate arrangements, short song lengths and catchy hook-oriented melodies. Although there are classic examples of soloing by Armenteros on the album, they are less numerous than on the other two Salsoul records. Armenteros does not solo on *Ya Mismo* and the cha cha cha *La Tierra de Sabor*. Most of his soloing on the up-tempo salsa songs is confined to the end of each piece. One example is *Castigador*, the first selection on the album. This is a remake of a minor hit previously recorded by Roberto Torres. Here Armenteros plays over the *moña* and *coro* sections at the end of the piece. His solo on the end of *Dejeme tranquilo* is a dynamic showcase of trumpet performance virtuosity. He also plays solos at the end of *Mulato* and *Barco Sin Rumbo*. Both songs are in a minor key, a trend that pervades all of the Salsoul sides. His solo work on *Barco Sin Rumbo* is some of the best on the album. Another highlight is *Para Que Aprendas*, which is a *guajira*. Armenteros is famous for his *guajira* playing; almost every recording and public performance by the trumpet player includes at least one *guajira*. He plays long solos both at the beginning and ending parts of *Para Que Aprendas*. *El Gordito de Oro* features an extended *largo* and a laidback trumpet solo, while *Un Caminante Con Salsa* features a lengthy solo over *moñas* and *coros* in the Eddie Palmieri mode.

Chocolate Caliente was recorded approximately a year later than *Juntos* and contains many similarities. Except for the American rhythm and blues influenced *Hot Chocolate*, the songs are a mixture of medium tempo *son montunos*, boleros, and the requisite *guajira (Guajira Inspiracíon)*. *Estoy Enamorado* and *Comprension* are both boleros and contain a minimal amount of improvised solo playing, although there is some fine lead and solo melody playing by Armenteros. Four of the medium tempo salsa/*son montuno* numbers (*Retozon, Sigan La Clave, Nicolaso* and *Que Sepa*) are in a minor key; Armenteros plays outstanding solos on *Sigan La Clave* and

Nicolaso. Another example of the mature Armenteros at his best is his soloing on the opening *La Mula*, which is based on a continuous dominant-seventh harmony and a two-three clave. Although there are many similarities between *Juntos* and *Chocolate Caliente*, the latter lacks some of the production values of *Juntos* and sounds less commercial. At times there are severe intonation problems within the horn section, and the neo-*búgalu* *Hot Chocolate* suffers in the test of time with its mid-1970s American pop music associations. However, the songs on *Juntos* tend to be more commercially oriented than the selections on *Chocolate Caliente*; at times *Juntos* suffers from an overly cute sentimentality.

Armenteros's final Salsoul album, *Chocolate en El Rincon*, was released in 1976 and contains two distinct components. The first five selections are similar in concept and personnel to *Juntos* and *Chocolate Caliente*. However, the final four pieces are in the descarga mode and feature a different group of musicians. These musicians include all-star salseros Andy González on bass and percussionist Manny Oquendo. The first part of *Chocolate En El Rincón* contains a typical salsa/*conjunto* format with sonero Willie Garcia and a four-piece horn section. Following a trend on the two earlier albums, the first two selections are both minor key straight-ahead salsa songs. *Controlate* features a typical call-and-response section between trumpet and *coro* as well as an Armenteros solo over *moña* and *coro* at the end. *Sé Tu Historia* follows a similar format with a two-measure minor key *montuno* pattern. *Lo Dicen Todas* is an Arsenio Rodríguez composition, played Eddie Palmieri-style, with a piano solo and a *moña*/trumpet solo section. *Aprietala En El Rincón* is a I-IV-V *montuno* from beginning to end; Armenteros plays continuously over the first part of the piece and again in the *moña* section. *Inocencia* is a bolero and the final song on the first part of the album. Armenteros plays a beautiful interpretation of the song's melody toward the end of the piece.

Trumpet En Montuno, a minor key *son*-based descarga, initially features Armenteros trading *montuno* sections with the initial four-bar *coro*. Later the trumpet/*coro* call-and-response is shortened to two-measure sections before a final fadeout section that contains only solo trumpet and rhythm section. *La cayuga* is an unusual instrumental danzón-*montuno*. The first part of the tune is an Orestes López danzón with Armenteros performing the vocal melody. One of the earliest of modern Cuban music styles, the danzón predates the *son* and is usually associated with flutes and violins and not the septeto trumpet. This is probably why the *montuno* section contains the improvised portion of Armenteros's playing on the piece. *Chocolate en ti* is an instrumental jam session over a one-chord medium slow tempo *tumbao*. For some reason, the piece is divided into two different selections on the album, although both appear to be part of the same recording. Armenteros performs a lengthy, slowly developed solo during *Chocolate en ti* (part 1). Part 2 fades in with a piano solo, which is followed by a bongo solo and a bass solo. The piece ends with rambunctious soloing by Armenteros.

SAR

Starting in 1980, Armenteros joined SAR Records, which was owned by Roberto Torres (Armenteros's partner on the earlier Salsoul recording *Juntos*). Torres produced three of Armenteros's recordings on SAR. Like the previous Salsoul series, these recordings are firmly in the *conjunto* mode with a large horn section and full-blown vocals. Armenteros is featured prominently throughout the three volumes, albeit in a conservative *típico* format. The first two albums, *Prefiero el Son* and *Y Sigo con mi Son*, were re-released on CD as *Lo Mejor De Chocolate, Volumes 1 and 2*. *Prefiero el Son* was released in 1980 and featured, among others, José Rodrigues and Leopoldo Pineda on trombone and pianist Alfredo Valdéz, Jr. Rodrigues is the only trombonist on *Y Sigo con mi Son* (released in 1981), and the sonero is Fernando Lavoy. Aside from Tony Divan (lead singer on *Prefiero el Son*), all other personnel is the same on both albums. The third SAR album, *Chocolate Dice*, was released in 1982 and has a number of personnel changes. Most significant is the trombone section, which in this case contains veteran Lewis Kahn and a young Jimmy Bosch.

The formal characteristics of the SAR recordings are similar to the Salsoul recordings. In particular, the production values of *Juntos* are present in these Torres-produced recordings. Because of the formal similarities between the Salsoul and SAR recordings, the SAR recordings will not be discussed in detail. Although a thorough analysis is beyond our purpose, these recordings should and ideally will be subjected to a more rigorous examination in the future. Suffice it to say that there are many outstanding salsa pieces on these three volumes, as well as some excellent soloing by Armenteros.

CAIMAN

Switching to an all-instrumental format, Armenteros recorded three albums for the Caiman label. *Chocolate En Sexteto* was released in 1983 followed by *¡Rompiendo Hielo!* in 1984. *Chocolate y Amigos* was recorded around the same time, but was not released until several years later. These three albums contain some of the most extended and exciting solo playing by Armenteros on record. Based on a more freewheeling and improvisational approach than utilized on most of his previous recordings, Armenteros's playing on the Caiman works extends the trumpet soloing concepts that he had developed in the 1970s on the Eddie Palmieri and Grupo Folklórico albums. Besides Armenteros, these three albums also feature Mario

Rivera on baritone saxophone and flute, and future "salsa romántica" producing mogul Sergio George on piano.

Although the Salsoul and SAR recordings are very similar in terms of formal characteristics, the three Caiman instrumental recordings represent a major change in musical conception and approach. The descarga performances on the second half of *Chocolate En El Rincon* foreshadow the descarga style of the Caiman recordings, yet the rest of the selections on the Salsoul and SAR albums are in the mainstream vocal-oriented salsa realm. Two of the three albums Armenteros recorded on Caiman in the mid-1980s (*Chocolate En Sexteto* and (*Chocolate y Amigos*) are currently available in CD form; *¡Rompiendo de Hielo!* has yet to be re-released. Comments here will focus on the two available volumes.

There are three basic formal types used on *Chocolate En Sexteto* and *Chocolate y Amigos*. One type is the descarga, which predominates on *Chocolate En Sexteto*. A second type of piece is the instrumental interpretation of a standard song from the Afro-Cuban tradition. This practice is most prevalent on *Chocolate y Amigos*. The final song type is the instrumental bolero.

Four of the six selections on *Chocolate En Sexteto* are straight out descargas authored by Armenteros. Two of the four descargas are remakes of pieces recorded previously on the Grupo Folklorico albums. *Chocolate's Guajira* is a very loose interpretation of *Choco's Guajira* on volume one of the Grupo Folklórico set. Although this recording lacks the vocal *coro* of the original, much of the initial trumpet melody is identical. On this recording the piano plays the *guajeo* instead of the tres on the original. The second version is also faster in tempo than the Grupo Folklórico original.

The other remake is the guaguancó *Trompeta En Cueros*, which was originally included on the second Grupo Folklórico volume. In this case, the similarities are greater than in the two versions of the *guajira*. Armenteros begins both versions of *Trompeta En Cueros* with a rubato solo. He plays completely solo on the Grupo Folklórico rendition; on the *Chocolate En Sexteto* version he plays over a series of out-of-tempo percussion figures. In both cases, the initial solo section (similar on both recordings) is followed by a continuation of the trumpet solo over a percussion rumba sans bass and chordal instruments. At the end of this section, Armenteros plays the *coro* melody and brings in the rest of the ensemble. On the original, the *coro* comes in with the same melody and initiates a call-and-response section with the trumpeter. On the *Chocolate En Sexteto* version both horns perform the initial *coro* figure and Mario Rivera plays the second (and final) *coro* on baritone saxophone before Armenteros goes completely solo. The original recording features a tres solo instead of the Sergio George piano solo of the Caiman remake. Instead of trading with the *coro* toward the end of the piece, as on the Grupo Folklórico version, Armenteros trades solo sections with Rivera. The other two descargas on *Chocolate En Sexteto* are both *son montunos* written by Armenteros. Both *Montuno Caliente* and *Trompeta en Montuno* contain extended soloing by members of the band.

A second type of composition featured on the Caiman recordings is the traditional Afro-Cuban standard. This type of piece is represented on *Chocolate En Sexteto* by the *son-pregon El Manicero* (The Peanut Vendor), which was an internationally popular success in the 1930s. There are three Afro-Cuban standards on *Chocolate y Amigos. Son de La Loma* is one of the most famous Cuban songs and was originally recorded in the early 1920s by the seminal *son* group Trio Matamoros. Likewise, *Guantanamera* and *La Macarena* are standard songs that are recognized not just by Latin Americans but throughout the world. Although there are many descarga elements present in these renditions of Cuban standards, the lyricism of Armenteros is showcased in his inventive interpretations of these famous melodies.

Mi Sentir on *Chocolate En Sexteto* is a rhythmic *bolero-beguine*, while the two boleros on *Chocolate y Amigos* feature sophisticated synthesizer-based arrangements by Sergio George in a preview of his future career as a star making producer for RMM and other commercial Latin music labels.

Armenteros's work as a featured sideman on these and other labels during the same time period is equally impressive. In addition to pursuing his own projects, Armenteros spent much of the late 1970s traveling the world with Sonora Mantancera; following this tenure, Armenteros joined Machito's band for most of the 1980s. Among the recordings he performed on during the 1970s was *With a Touch of Brass* (1974) by the New York band Típica Novel. While on tour in Venezuela with Sonora Mantancera in 1979, Armenteros recorded *Se Empató el Sonero* with Sonero Clasico del Caribe, which consisted of a number of veteran Venezuelan musicians who specialized in the Cuban *son*/septeto style. In a departure, Armenteros lent his authentic Caribbean trumpet styling to a calypso record album entitled *Knockdown Calypso '79* by Trinidad veteran Growling Tiger. In the 1980s, Armenteros performed as a sideman on numerous albums. He appeared with Machito on three albums recorded in 1982 and 1983 in conjunction with an historic series of appearances by the band in London during the early 1980s. Departing from his normal salsa context, Armenteros appeared with an American jazz group on pianist Cedar Walton's *Eastern Rebellion 4*, which featured noted jazz trombonist Curtis Fuller. Aside from his work as a leader, Armenteros recorded prolifically on the Caiman label as a sideman during the 1980s. Among the recordings was *Super All-Star '84*, which featured an all-star lineup including Tito Puente and Paquito D'Rivera. In a more traditional mode, he recorded on *Pionero Del Son* with Alfredo Valdés, Sr., in 1984 and on *Con Tumbao* with Los Guaracheros de Oriente.[22]

CHOCOLATE: ELDER STATESMAN

In the late 1980s and early 1990s, legendary Cuban bassist Israel Cachao López made an impressive reappearance on the Afro-Cuban musical scene. In addition to recording a two-volume set of Grammy award-winning CDs entitled *Master Sessions, I and II* in 1995, López and his cast of characters filmed a documentary, *Como Su Ritmo No Hay Dos*, which was produced and directed by actor Andy Garcia. The group included both younger musicians (trombonist Jimmy Bosch and saxophonist Paquito D'Rivera) and veterans (Armenteros and pianist Alfredo Valdéz, Jr.). Cachao also revived the traditional danzón and the charanga with this group. In fact, this ensemble was two bands in one with instrumental changes made to reflect either the danzón or the *son* tradition. When a danzón was performed, the ensemble included a string section and the flutist Nestor Torres. A horn section replaced these players when a descarga was performed. Like the members of Grupo Folklórico in the mid-1970s and the Cuban purists of the early salsa era, Cachao's goal was to create an Afro-Cuban renaissance. Armenteros' trumpet playing on these Lopez dates was one of the crucial elements in providing authenticity to this charanga/*conjunto*/descarga recreation. His junior colleague on trombone, Jimmy Bosch, proved his own firm grasp of the "Chocolate" style. Although Armenteros was in his sixties by the time these recordings were made, age obviously had had little deleterious effect on the trumpet master's performing prowess.

As the twenty-first century begins, and Armenteros enters his seventh decade, the trumpeter remains very active. Following on the major success of López's *Master Sessions* CDs and documentary film in the mid-1990s, Armenteros recorded two CDs with the Caiman label all-star group, the Estrellas Caiman. Both CDs feature top salsa stars under the musical direction of pianist Alfredo Valdéz, Jr. The first CD, *Descarga in New York* (Estrellas Caiman), was released in 1995 and features, among other selections, an Armenteros interpretation of the Kurt Weill standard *Mack the Knife*, which the trumpeter had previously recorded on *¡Rompiendo de Hielo!* from his Caiman period. *Descarga del Milenio* (Estrellas Caiman), released in 1997, is a slicker production, featuring most of the same performers plus a string section. This second volume is less swinging and freewheeling than the initial recording.

Armenteros is featured prominently on trombonist Jimmy Bosch's first recording as a leader, *Soneando Trombón*, released in 1998 on the Rykolatino label. The year 1998 also marked the first release in a number of years of a new Armenteros-led recording; entitled *Chocolate and His Latin Soul*, the Caiman CD is an instrumental compendium featuring a front line of trumpet and a four-man saxophone section.

The latest generation of Cuba-based musicians and groups did not exist when Armenteros left Cuba. Many of the top musicians on the current

Cuban scene weren't even born when Armenteros departed four decades ago. "When I left it was all about Arsenio, René Alvarez, Arcaño y sus Maravillas, Beny Moré, Melodias del Cuarenta, La Orquesta Ideal de Joseito. These other fellows [Jésus Alemañy, Los Van Van, etc.] weren't around yet."[23] His opinion of current Afro-Cuban/salsa trumpet players is that they are deficient in originality and individual identity. Two exceptions are Luis "Perico" Ortiz and Jésus Alemañy. Armenteros has high regards for the well-rounded musicianship of producer/composer/trumpeter Ortiz. As for Alemañy, Armenteros admires the young trumpet player's respect for tradition and states that "he's one of the musicians that preserves the style pretty well."[24] Armenteros enjoys the Cuban genres such as the songo and timba that have been created by newer Cuban musicians and is happy that the younger bands are often using traditional instruments such as the batá drums.

At the end of the twentieth century, Alfredo "Chocolate" Armenteros actively and proudly maintains his position as the most important of all Afro-Cuban/salsa trumpet players. In addition to numerous other engagements, on the first Monday of every month Armenteros can be found at Willie's Steak House beneath the elevated IRT #6 train on Westchester Avenue in the Bronx. As regular guest soloist with pianist Willie Rodríguez's house band, Armenteros continues to be a living tribute to the Afro-Cuban septeto trumpet tradition.

Appendix: Album Titles

MONGO SANTAMARÍA

Tambores Afro-Cubanos 1953 SMC

Chango 1953 Tico

Drums and Chants 1955 (compilation of the preceding two recordings), Vaya

Yambú 1959 Fantasy

Mongo 1959 Fantasy

Afro-Roots (compilation of the preceding two recordings) 1972, 1997CD Prestige

Our Man in Havana 1960, 1993CD Fantasy

Bembe 1960 Fantasy

Our Man in Havana (compliation of the preceding two recordings) 1993 Fantasy

¡Sabroso! Charanga y Pachanga, 1961 Fantasy (1993CD Original Jazz Classics)

¡Arriba! La Pachanga 1962, 1996CD Fantasy

Mas Sabroso 1962 Fantasy

¡Viva Mongo! 1962 Fantasy

Mighty Mongo 1962 Fantasy

At the Blackhawk 1962, 1994CD Fantasy

Go Mongo 1962 Riverside

Mongo Introduces La Lupe 1963 Riverside (1993CD Milestone)

Watermelon Man! 1963 Battle (1993CD BGP)

Mongo at the Village Gate 1963 Battle, 1990CD Original Jazz Classics

The Watermelon Man (compilation of the preceding two recordings) 1973 Milestone

Mongo Explodes 1964 Riverside

Skins 1976, 1990CD (compilation of *Go Mongo!* and *Mongo Explodes*) Milestone

El Pussy Cat 1965 Columbia

La Bamba 1966 Columbia

El Bravo! 1966 Columbia

Hey! Let's Party 1966 Columbia

Mongomania 1967 Columbia

Explodes at the Village Gate 1967 Columbia

Soul Bag 1968 Columbia

Stone Soul 1969 Columbia

Workin' on a Groovy Thing 1969 Columbia

All Strung Out 1969 Columbia

Feelin' Alright 1970 Atlantic

Mongo 1970 Atlantic

Mongo's Way 1971 Atlantic

Mongo at Montreux 1971 Atlantic

Up from the Roots 1972 Atlantic

Fuego 1973, 1996CD Vaya

Live at Yankee Stadium 1974 Vaya

Afro-Indio 1975 Vaya

Mongo & Justo "Ubane" 1976 Vaya

Sofrito 1976 Vaya

Amanacer 1977 Vaya

A La Carte 1978, 1996CD Vaya

Mongo Mongo 1978, 1997CD Vaya

Red Hot 1979 CBS Images, 1980 Vaya

Images with Dizzy Gillespie 1980 Vaya

Mambo Mongo: Fania Super Hits 1977, 1994CD Fania

Summertime 1980 Pablo

Mongo Magic 1983 Roulette

Free Spirit 1985 Tropical Buddah

Soy Yo 1987, 1995CD Concord Picante

Greatest Hits 1988 Sony

Soca Me Nice 1988 Concord Picante

Olé Olá 1989 Concord Picante

Live at Jazz Alley 1990 Concord Picante
Brazilian Sunset 1992 Candid
Mambo Mongo 1993 Chesky
Mongo Returns 1995 Milestone

Sideman Recordings and Collections

Camilo, Michel: *Michel Camillo* 1988 Portrait/CBS

Capers, Valerie: *Come on Home* 1995 Columbia

Fania All-Stars: *Rhythm Machine* 1977 Fania

Feldman, Victor: *Latinsville* 1959 Contemporary

Gasca, Luis: *The Little Giant* 1969 Atlantic

Latin Music Legends: *Mambo Show* 1985 Tropical Buddha

Loco, Joe: *Pachanga with Joe Loco* 1961 Fantasy, *Loco Motion* 1961 Fantasy

Morales, Noro: *Recordando los Exitos, Vol. 1* 1954–56 RCA/BMG

Puente, Tito: *El Timbal* 1949–51 Greycliff, *The Best of Tito Puente Vol. 1* 1955 RCA/BMG, *Puente in Percussion* 1955 Tico, *Cuban Carnival* 1955–56 RCA/BMG, *Mucho Puente* 1955–57 RCA/BMG, *Cubarama* 1956 RCA/BMG, *Puente Goes Jazz* 1956 RCA/BMG, *Yambeque* 1955–57 RCA/BMG, *Top Percussion* 1957 RCA/BMG, *Night Beat* 1957 RCA/BMG

Puente, Tito and the Golden Latin All-Stars: *In Session* 1993 Tropijazz

Prado, Perez: *Al Compás del Mambo 1950–52* Tumbao

Ruiz, Hilton: *Strut* 1988 RCA/Novus

Sanchez, Poncho: *Conga Blue* 1995 Concord Picante

Tjader, Cal: *Ritmo Caliente* 1955 Fantasy, *Más Ritmos Caliente* 1955 Fantasy, *Cal Tjader Quintet* 1956–57 Fantasy, *Cal Tjader Goes Latin* 1958 Fantasy, *Latin Concert* 1958 Fantasy/OJC, *Latin for Lovers* 1958 Fantasy, *Sentimental Moods* 1958 Fantasy, *Black Orchid* 1959 Fantasy, *Concerts by the Sea Vol. 1 and 2* 1959 Prestige/OJC, *Monterey Concerts* 1959 Prestige/OJC, *A Night at the Black-hawk* 1959 Fantasy, *Live and Direct* 1959 Fantasy, *Demesiado Caliente!* 1960 Fantasy, *Latino!* 1960 Fantasy, *Concert on the Campus* 1960 Fantasy, *West Side Story* 1960 Fantasy

Turre, Steve: *Steve Turre* 1997 Verve

JÉSUS CAUNEDO

Fire and Sugar 1973 Montilla
Puerto Rican Jazz 1986 Gema

Sideman Recordings and Collections

De los Reyes, Walfredo: *Cuban Jazz* 1960 Gema/Palladium

D'Rivera, Paquito: *40 Years of Cuban Jam Session* 1993 Messidor

Gutierrez, Julio: *Progressive Latin* c. 1970 Gema

Machito: *The New Sound of Machito* 1962 Tico

Puente, Tito: *El Excitante Ritmo* 1963 Tico, *Mucho, Mucho Puente* 1964 Tico, *De Mí Para Tí* 1964 Tico, *My Fair Lady Goes Latin* 1964 Roulette, *Tito Swings. The Exciting La Lupe Sings* 1965 Tico, *Carnival in Harlem* 1966 Tico

FÉLIX "PUPI" LEGARRETA

Salsa Nova (New Spice) 1962 Tico (reissued 1976 Fania and retitled *Toda la Verdad*)

Pupi y su Charanga 1975 Fania/Vaya

Pupi y Pacheco: Los Dos Mosqueteros—The Two Musketeers 1977 Fania/Vaya

El Fugitivo 1979 Fania/Vaya

Pupi Pa' Bailar 1980 Fania/Vaya

Sideman Recordings and Collections

Cachao y su Descarga: *Vol. 1* 1976 Salsoul, *Dos* 1977 Salsoul

Calzado, Rudy: *Rica Charanga* 1986 Caiman

Fania All-Stars: *Havana Jam* 1979 Fania

Fernández, Don Gonzalo: *Super Típica de Estrellas* 1976 All-Art

Harlow, Larry: *El Judio Maravilloso* 1975 Fania, *Con Mi Viejo Amigo* 1976 Fania, *El Jardinero Del Amor* 1976 Fania, *La Raza Latina* 1977 Fania, *El Albino Divino* 1978 Fania

Orquesta Son Primero: *Charanga—Tradición Cubana en Neuva York* 1987 Montuno

Pacheco, Johnny: *Pacheco, His Flute and Latin Jam* 1965 Fania

Torres, Roberto: *Presenta: Ritmo de Estrellas* 1980 Guajiro

Vasquez, Javier y su Charanga: *Tres Flautas* 1980 Fania

JUAN PABLO TORRES

¡Y Viva la Felicidad! 1972 Egrem

Mangle 1973 Egrem

Super Son 1974 Egrem

Con Todos los Hierros 1977 Egrem
Pan Caliente c. 1981 Golden
Grupo Algo Nuevo c. 1982 Egrem
Algo Nuevo 1983 Areito
Yamina c. 1987 Areito
Trombone Man 1995 Tropijazz
Pepper Trombone 1997 Tropijazz
Descarga Afro-Cubana 1998 Caiman

Sideman Recordings and Collections

Descarga Boricua II 1995 Tropijazz

D'Rivera, Paquito: *40 Years of Cuban Jam Session* 1993 Messidor, *Cuba Jazz* 1995 Tropijazz

Estrellas Areito (Reissued by World Circuit 1999 and retitled *Los Heroes*)

Orquesta Cubana de Musica Moderna: *Cuba qué Linda es Cuba* 1968 Areito, *Directo Desde Cuba* 1969 Areito

Orquesta Típica: *En Cuba Intercambio Cultural* 1973 Fania

Torres, Nestor: *Talk to Me* 1996 Sony

Torres, Roberto: *Fiesta* 1996 SAR

Tropijazz All-Stars, Vols. 1 & 2 1996 Tropijazz

Valdés, Bebo: *Bebo Rides Again* 1994 Messidor

JUAN-CARLOS FORMELL

Songs from a Little Blue House 1999 Wicklow (BMG Classics)

Sideman Recordings and Collections

The Latin Lullaby 1997 Ellipsis Arts

ALFREDO "CHOCOLATE" ARMENTEROS

Chocolate and His Cuban Soul 1998 Caiman
Chocolate Aquí 1994 Carib Musicana
Chocolate Caliente 1998 Salsoul
Chocolate en Sexteto n.d. Caiman
Chocolate y Amigos n.d. Caiman

Lo Mejor de Chocolate, Volume 1 1990 SAR
Lo Mejor de Chocolate, Volume 2 1991 SAR

Sideman Recordings and Collections

Chapotín, Félix and Alfredo "Chocolate" Armenteros: *Estrellas de Cuba* n.d. Antilla

Estrellas Caiman: *Descarga in New York* 1995 Caiman, *Descarga del Milenio* 1997 Caiman

Lopez, Israel Cachao: *Cachao Master Sessions Volume I and II* 1995 Crescent Moon/Epic

Palmieri, Eddie: *Justicia* 1970 Tico, *Super-Imposition* 1970 Tico, *Vamanos Paíl Monte* 1976 Tico

Rodríguez, Arsenio: *Dundunbanza* 1994 Tumbao

Other Recordings Cited in Chapter 11

Alemañy, Jesús: *Jes's Alemañy's Cubanismo!* 1996 Root Jazz/Hannibal

Blades, Ruben: *Antecedente* 1988 Elektra/Asylum

Chapotín, Félix: *Chapotín y sus Estrellas* n.d. Antilla, *Perlas del Son* n.d. Areito, *Sabor Tropical* n.d. Ruchito

Cuní, Miguelito: *Sones de Ayer* n.d. Rumba Records

Dorham, Kenny: *Afro-Cuban* 1955 Blue Note

D'Rivera, Paquito: *Paquito DíRivera Presents CubaJazz* 1996 TropiJazz/RMM

Gillespie, Dizzy: *Compact Jazz: Dizzy Gillespie* 1987 PolyGram

Palmieri, Eddie: *Azucar Pa' Ti (Sugar For You)* 1965 Tico, *Bamboleate* 1967 Tico, *Champagne* 1968 Tico, *Echando Paílante (Straight Ahead)* 1964 Tico, *El Molestoso* 1962 Alegre, *La Perfecta* 1962 Alegre, *Lo Que Traigo Es Sabrosa* 1964 Alegre, *Molasses* 1967 Tico, *Mozambique* 1965 Tico

Sexteto Habanero: *The Roots of Salsa, Volume II* n.d. Folklyric Records

Notes

INTRODUCTION

1. George Rivera, "Q&A: A Conversation with Johnny Almendra and Jillian," http://www.jazzconclave.com/atm.htm.

CHAPTER 1

1. Joyce LaFray, *¡Cuba Cocina! The Tantalizing World of Cuban Cooking—Yesterday, Today and Tomorrow* (New York: Hearst Books, 1994), p. 3.

2. Trombonist Juan Pablo Torres told me that he knew little about Afro-Cuban jazz before he moved to the United States in the early 1990s. [Juan Pablo Torres, interview at his home in Union City, New Jersey, July 1999.]

3. Steven Loza, *Tito Puente and the Making of Latin Music* (Urbana and Chicago: University of Illinois Press, 1999), p. 89.

4. Ibid., p. 165.

5. Ibid., p. 152. Other Cuban-style singers who are not of Cuban descent are Jose "El Canario" Beltran from the Dominican Republic, the Venezuelan bandleader Oscar D'Leon and the Puerto Rican Marvin Santiago.

6. Willie Colón, rec.music.afro-latin (newsgroup) (April 1, 1998).

7. Gustavo Pérez Firmat, *Life on the Hyphen: The Cuban-American Way* (Austin: University of Texas Press, 1994), pp. 104–5.

8. Silvana Paternostro, interview of Juan Formell, *Bomb* (Winter 2000): 120–23.

9. Sue Steward, "Daniel Ponce," *The Wire* (July 1985): 22.

10. David Garcia, telephone interview, October 1999.

11. Financial restrictions are placed on cultural exchanges with Cuba. None of

the money generated by concert revenues is permitted to go to the Cuban government. See Mireya Navarro, "Famed Cuban Band Is Set to Perform in Miami, and the Overtone is One of Strain," *New York Times* (October 9, 1999), p. A10.

12. Art Levine, "Viva Buena Vista Social Club," www.salon.com.

13. Silvana Paternostro, "Juan Formell," *Bomb* (Winter 2000): 123. According to Paternostro, the name of the group has entered into common Cuban slang. To say something is really good, people say: "It's a *van van.*" (Ibid.)

14. Ibid.

15. David Cázares, "Vintage Reunion," *South Florida Sun Sentinel* (November 27, 1998).

CHAPTER 2

1. Frank M. Figueroa, "Mario Bauzá: Highlights from his Smithsonian Jazz Oral History Interview," posted on Picadillo.com. (n.d.).

2. Max Salazar, "Remembering Marcelino "Rapindey" Guerra," *Latin Beat Magazine 10/3* (April 2000): 31.

3. See Susan D. Greenbaum, "Tampa, Florida, 1886–1984," in *Tampa Bay History: Journal of the University of South Florida Department of History*, 1995.

4. Mossa Bildner, telephone interview, April 2000.

5. Robin D. Moore, *Nationalizing Blackness: Afrocubaismo and Artistic Revolution in Havana, 1920–1940* (Pittsburgh: University of Pittsburgh Press, 1997), p. 15.

6. Ibid., p. 34.

7. Evaristo M. Martínez-Martínez, Internet posting, Yahoo! Message Boards: Buena Vista Social Club, June 26, 1999.

8. Frank M. Figueroa, "Mario Bauzá: Highlights from his Smithsonian Jazz Oral History Interview," www.picadillo.com/figueroa/bauza (n.d.).

9. Ibid.

10. Arnold Jay Smith, "Cuban King of Congas," *Downbeat Magazine* (April 21, 1977): 48.

CHAPTER 3

1. Mongo Santamaría, Interview at his home in New York City, July 1999.

2. "In Cuba, the exploitation of man by man has disappeared, and racial discrimination has disappeared too." Fidel Castro, cited in Lee Lockwood, *Castro's Cuba, Cuba's Fidel: An American Journalist's Inside Look at Today's Cuba* (New York: Vintage Books, 1969), p. 216.

3. "Soroa99," Internet posting, Yahoo! Message Board: Buena Vista Social Club, July 5, 1999.

4. Arnold Jay Smith, "Cuban King of Congas," *Downbeat Magazine* (April 21, 1977): 19.

5. *Cuba: I am Time* booklet, p. 99.

6. Anonymous, "Un balsero sin pelos en la lengua" *El Nacional* (Caracas, Venezuela, February 22, 2000).

7. Arturo Sandoval, telephone interview, July 1999.

8. Liz Balmaseda, "Spy Case Boosts Worst Suspicions—It Felt like Havana Deja vu. Request Denied. Request Denied. Request Denied," *Miami Herald*, February 21, 2000, p. 9.

9. Daniel Chang, "Sandoval's Passions," *The Orange County Register*, February 25, 2000.

10. Ibid.

11. Ibid.

12. Ricardo L. Ortíz, "Cuba, Culpa, and Albita Rodríguez's Exilt Desires," http://www.us.net/cuban/albita.htm.

13. Keith Raether, "Rubalcaba Finds a Home Beyond Cuba," *Seattle Post-Intelligencer*, October 22, 1999.

14. Both are discussed in detail later in this book.

CHAPTER 4

1. Norbert Goldberg, "An Interview with Mongo Santamaría," *Percussive Notes* (July 1998): 56.

2. Mongo Santamaría, interview, Smithsonian Institution Jazz Oral History Program, 1996. Translated by Mossa Bildner.

3. Robin D. Moore thinks "that any offhand reference to Amalia by a Cuban is probably talking about Amalia Batista, a famous and semimythical mulatta figure who was the subject of a book and also a big zarzuela production written by Rodrigo Prats." (E-mail to the author, November 1999).

4. Mongo Santamaría, interview, Smithsonian Institution Jazz Oral History Program, 1996.

5. Hugh Thomas, *Cuba: Or the Pursuit of Freedom* (New York: Da Capo Press, 1998), pp. 516–17.

6. David W. Ames, "Negro Family Types in a Cuban Solar," *Phylon 11* no. 2 (1950): 161.

7. Ibid., p. 163.

8. Mongo Santamaría, interview at his home in New York City, July 1999.

9. Ames, "Negro Family Types in a Cuban Solar," p. 159.

10. Mongo Santamaría, interview at his home in New York City, July 1999.

11. Arnold J. Smith, "Mongo Santamaría: Cuban King of Congas," *Downbeat* (April 21, 1977): 19.

12. Gonzalo Martré, *Rumberos de Ayer: Musicos Cubanos en Mexico 1930 a 1950* (Veracruz, Mexico: Instituto Veracruzano de Cultura, 1997), p. 48.

13. Moore, *Nationalizing Blackness*, p. 276.

14. The dance developed in a little hamlet called Columbia near the village of Union de Reyes in rural Matanzas (Martré, *Rumberos de Ayer*, p. 27). Some columbia dancers use knives that they thrust across the body and under the arms, left-right-left-right, in a dangerously rapid movement. Rumba columbia has its roots in abakua, the fraternal society that many musicians, including some of Santamaría's associates, have belonged to.

15. Miguel Barnet, *Biography of a Runaway Slave*, translated by W. Nick Hill (Willimantic, Conn.: Curbstone Press, 1994), pp. 76–77.

16. Joseph M. Murphy, *Santeria: African Spirits in America* (Boston: Beacon Press, 1988), p. 27.

17. An alternative explanation for the term stems from an ancient port of Ulkami or Lucumi in the south of Nigeria.

18. Moore, *Nationalizing Blackness*, p. 31.

19. John Mason, *Orin Orisa: Songs for Selected Heads* (New York: Yoruba Center, 1992), p. 18. Aguabella's religious name is Olufundeii: "the Lord caused this one to be crowned" (Mason, *Orin Orisa*, p. 18). He was born in Matanzas in 1925. After moving to Havana, he played in a group with Julito Collazo and Cándido Camero, a Cuban conguero who moved to the United States in the late 1940s. He was discovered by the African American dance ethnologist and choreographer Katherine Dunham. She took Collazo and Aguabella with her to Rome to appear in the movie *Mambo*, directed by Robert Rossen. Afterward, both drummers became members of her touring ensemble. In the United States, Aguabella recorded on Santamaría's first two records on the Fantasy label: *Yambú* and *Mongo*, and Santamaría brought his Cuban friend to the attention of Tito Puente. Both Aguabella and Collazo appeared along with Santamaría on Puente's album *Top Percussion*, an album that features Lucumí praise chants. He has performed and recorded with the top names of Latin music including Tito Puente, Eddie Palmieri and Cachao. In the jazz field, he has recorded with Barney Kessel, Louis Bellson and Dizzy Gillespie. Aguabella also has had a successful career in pop music performing regularly with Peggy Lee and Frank Sinatra. In the 1990s, Aguabella received a National Fellowship Award that recognized his accomplishments as a master of folkloric music. Documentary maker Les Blank made a film called *Sworn to the Drum* about the drummer, which reunited him with Julito Collazo. He is presently on the faculty of UCLA's ethnomusicology department. [Nat Chediak, *Diccionario de Jazz Latino* (Madrid: Edición de Fernando Trueba, 1998), pp. 16–17.]

20. Julito Collazo's name in the religion is Oba Funmillu Ayan: "The King gave me the drums of Ayan" (Mason, *Orin Orisa*, p. 18). He is featured on Santamaría's first album recorded under his own name: *Drum and Chants*, an album whose original title was *Chango*. Although Collazo worked for some of the top names in Latin music such as Machito, Puente and Eddie Palmieri, he never ventured far from the world of Santería, which he learned about as a small child since his mother, Ebelia Collazo, was a renowned Santera (Marta Moreno Vega, "The Yoruba Orisha Tradition Comes to New York City," *African American Review*, vol. 29, no. 2 [Summer, 1995]: 201). He has lived in New York City for many years, where he is regarded as an authority on many aspects of the religion. In addition to playing batá, he is onisango (priest of Chango). Among his students in the art of batá is Steve Berrios, a New York-born drummer who has played with Santamaría's groups on several occasions (Chediak, *Diccionario de Jazz Latino*, p. 36).

21. Mason, *Orin Orisa*, p. 19.

22. Yvonne Daniel, *Rumba: Dance and Social Change in Contemporary Cuba* (Bloominton and Indianapolis: University of Indiana Press, 1995), p. 78.

23. In the 1920s, the Orquesta Sinfónica de la Habana and the Orquesta Filharmónica were both founded. At least half of their respective members were Afro-Cubans (Moore, *Nationalizing Blackness*, p. 247, n44).

24. Mongo Santamaría, interview, Smithsonian Institution Jazz Oral History Program, 1996.

25. According to Armando Peraza, the instrument maker's name was Velgada [Trevor Salloum, *The Bongo Book* (Pacific, Mo: Mel Bay, 1996), p. 51].

26. Mongo Santamaría, interview, Smithsonian Institution Jazz Oral History Program, 1996.

27. Smith, "Mongo Santamaría: King of Congas," p. 48.

28. Goldberg, "An Interview with Mongo Santamaría," p. 55.

29. There are several New World musical genres with the name *son* appended to them: Mexico has *el son huasteco* and Guatemala, *el son chapín*. Composer Edgardo Martin states in his book *Panorama historico de la música en Cuba* that the word in this usage refers to a danceable song (*un canto bailable*) [cited by Erena Hernández, *La Música en Persona* (Havana: Editorial Letras Cubanas, 1986), p. 157].

30. Olga Fernández, *Strings and Hide* (Havana: Editorial José Martí, 1995), p. 88.

31. Erena Hernández, *La Música en Persona* (Havana: Editorial Letras Cubanas, 1986).

32. Ibid., p. 51.

33. Mongo Santamaría, interview, Smithsonian Institution Jazz Oral History Program, 1996.

34. Graham Greene, *Our Man in Havana* (London: Penguin, 1958), p. 83. Elizabeth Ruf, a dancer and theatrical scholar, studied the Tropicana in the 1990s, and her description of the famous nightspot adds considerably to Greene's peremptory report: "The tables are arranged in raked, concentric semicircular banks around a raised circular stage, and share the space with coconut palms, *mamoncillos* (a tropical fruit), tropical flowers, and birds. Structurally, the Tropicana theatre has much in common with the theatres of ancient Greece. Behind the circular orchestra is a rectangular skene area, a multi-level performance space more than ten meters high, consisting of a series of sculptural platforms and catwalks nestled into the fronds of the surrounding palms. The circular part of the performance area is mechanically lowered to ground level during the intermissions and the audience is invited to dance to recorded salsa music" [Elizabeth Ruf, "Issues of Gender, Color, and Nationalism in Cuba's Tropicana Nightclub Performance," *The Drama Review* 41, no. 1 (Spring 1997): 93].

35. Moore, *Nationalizing Blackness*, p. 186.

36. Ruf, "Issues of Gender, Color, and Nationalism in Cuba's Tropicana Nightclub Performance," p. 93.

37. Moore, *Nationalizing Blackness*, pp. 184–85.

38. Martré, *Rumberos de Ayer*, p. 48.

39. Smith, "Mongo Santamaría: Cuban King of Congas," p. 20.

40. Although Valdés's music is nearly forgotten today, he was once renowned for incorporating Afro-Cuban percussion into symphonic work and lavish stage productions. His music was endorsed by Beroff Mendietta, mayor of Havana, and the National Tourist Commission. It was performed in the Anfiteatro de la Habana, generating large amounts of money for the composer. A few performances were made free to the public because Mendietta believed that it was important "to put the masses in contact with correct interpretations of their own music." [Moore, *Nationalizing Blackness*, p. 83].

41. Verve Records VE2–2522. Originally recorded on Norgran, 1954. Dizzy Gillespie with Al Fraser, *To Be, Or No . . . to Bop: Memoirs* (Garden City, N.Y.: Doubleday & Co., 1979), p. 514.

42. Smith, "Mongo Santamaría: Cuban King of Congas," p. 20.

43. Mongo Santamaría, interview, Smithsonian Institution Jazz Oral History Program, 1996.

44. Ibid.

45. Ibid.

46. Armando Peraza, interview, Smithsonian Institution Jazz Oral History Program, 1994.

47. Smith, "Mongo Santamaría: Cuban King of Congas," p. 19.

48. Mongo Santamaría, interview at his home in New York City, July 1999.

49. Armando Peraza, interview, Smithsonian Institution Jazz Oral History Program, 1994.

50. Fernández, *Strings and Hide*, p. 87.

51. Hernández, *La Música en Persona*, p. 98.

52. Ibid., p. 99.

53. Moore, *Nationalizing Blackness*, p. 266, n29.

54. Ibid., pp. 99–100.

55. Ibid., p. 39.

56. The position of mailman was opened up to Afro-Cubans in 1912 (Barnet, *Biography of a Runaway Slave*, p. 195) as a means of assuaging the hatred of the Afro-Cuban community, which had suffered a terrible tragedy at the hand of the government. The Little War of 1912 (La Guerrita del Doce) an uprising of blacks who wanted their own political party based on race, had culminated in a vicious massacre (Moore, *Nationalizing Blackness*, p. 30).

57. Mongo Santamaría, interview, Smithsonian Institution Jazz Oral History Program, 1996.

58. Mongo Santamaría, interview at his home in New York City, July 1999.

59. Smith, "Mongo Santamaría: Cuban King of Congas," p. 19.

60. Mongo Santamaría, interview at his home in New York City, July 1999.

61. Matré, *Rumberos de Ayer*, p. 11.

62. Ibid., pp. 13–25.

63. Ibid., p. 24.

64. Mongo Santamaría, interview, Smithsonian Institution Jazz Oral History Program, 1996.

CHAPTER 5

1. *Santo* is a popular term for music and ritual connected with Santería.

2. Mongo Santamaría, interview at his home in New York City, July 1999.

3. Marta Moreno Vega, "The Yoruba Orisha Tradition Comes to New York City," *African American Review*, Vol. 29, no. 2 (Summer 1995): 202.

4. Joseph M. Murphy, *African Spirits in America* (Boston: Beacon Press, 1988), p. 50.

5. Max Salazar, "Machito: The Musician and the Root of New York's Latin Music," in *Caribe* (1984): pp. 38–40.

6. Pozo, like many other congueros, loved marijuana. But, although Nat Chediak (see next note) claims that his most famous song, *Manteca*, was the then-current slang word for marijuana, John Amira informed me that *manteca* has always referred to heroin, not to the magic weed (John Amira, interview at his home, New York City, October 1999).

7. Nat Chediak, *Diccionario de Jazz Latino* (Madrid: Edición de Fernando Trueba, Fundación Autor, 1998), pp. 180–81.

8. Mongo Santamaría, interview, Smithsonian Institution Jazz Oral History Program, 1996.

9. Luis Tamargo, "Mongo Santamaría: Refuting a Baseless Mythology," *Latin Beat*, vol. 1, no. 10 (November 1991): 12.

10. John Amira and Steven Cornelius. *The Music of Santería: Traditional Rhythms of the Batá Drums*. Crown Point, IN: White Cliffs Media, 1992.

11. The Iyesa drum ensemble consists of three drums, with a fourth drum added for certain *toques*. Iyesa drums are played with sticks.

12. John Mason, *Orin Orisa: Songs for Selected Heads* (New York: Yoruba Center, 1992), pp. 219–20.

13. Robin D. Moore, *Nationalizing Blackness: Afrocubanismo and Artistic Revolution in Havana, 1920–1940* (Pittsburgh: University of Pittsburgh Press, 1997), p. 278.

14. Frank M. Figueroa surmises that the *reales* were royal slaves. Frank M. Figueroa, *Glossary of Afro-Caribbean Terms* (Oldsmar, Fl: Pillar Publications, 1999). Robin Moore disagrees: "Virtually all the cabildos refered to themselves as *reales*. This was linked to the fact that they elected kings and queens and had an internal hierarchy build around these classifications, but there was nothing royal about them (Correspondence, March 2000).

15. Frank M. Figueroa, *Glossary of Afro-Caribbean Terms* (Oldsmar, Fl: Pillar Publications, 1999).

16. John Amira, interview at his home in New York City, October 1999.

17. Mason, *Orin Orisa*, pp. 411, 410, respectively.

18. Ibid., p. 315.

19. Philip Pasmanick, "Décima and Rumba: Iberian Formalism in the Heart of Afro-Cuban Song," *Latin American Music Review* vol. 4 (July 1997).

20. Moore, *Nationalizing Blackness*, p. 263, n42.

21. For a fascinating account of the mulata figure in Cuban culture, see Vera M. Kutzinski, *Sugar's Secrets: Race and the Erotics of Cuban Nationalism* (Charlottesville and London: University Press of Virginia, 1993).

22. Mongo Santamaría, interview at his home in New York City, July 1999.

23. Ibid.

24. Victor Rendón, "Mongo Santamaría on: Ti Mon Bo," *Latin Percussion Newsletter* (June 1995): 5.

25. Dick Hadlock. Liner notes to *Yambú*. Fantasy Records, 1959.

26. Mason, *Orin Orisa*, p. 355, 21A.

27. Ibid., p. 314.

28. Mary Overby, brochure for Grupo Afrocuba de Matanzas, http://metalab.unc.edu/mao/musicians/afrocubamore.

29. "toca constantemente el mismo ritmo básico para que el 'diablito' dance." Fernando Ortiz, *La Africanía de la Música Folklórica de Cuba* (Havana: Publicaciones Del Minestero de Educacion, 1950. Reprinted Madrid: Editorial Música Mundana Maqueda, SL, 1998), p. 169.

30. Yvonne Daniel, *Rumba: Dance and Social Change in Contemporary Cuba* (Bloomington and Indianapolis: University of Indiana Press, 1995), p. 87.

31. Birger Sulsbrück notes that playing sticks on bongos is an effective soloistic technique. The sticks used are shortened timbale sticks. *Latin-American Percussion: Rhythms and Rhythm Instruments from Cuba and Brazil* (English revised version, Copenhagen: Den Rytmiske Aftenskoles Forlag/Edition Wilhelm Hansen, 1986), p. 30.

32. Mason, *Orin Orisa*, p. 10ff.

33. Moore, *Nationalizing Blackness*, pp. 223–24.

34. Mongo Santamaría, interview, Smithsonian Institution Jazz Oral History Program, 1996.

35. Mongo Santamaría, interview at his home in New York City, July 1999.

CHAPTER 6

1. Mongo Santamaría, interview at his home in New York City, July 1999.

2. Mongo Santamaría, interview, Smithsonian Institution Jazz Oral History Program, 1996.

3. Ibid.

4. Arnold Jay Smith, "Mongo Santamaría: Cuban King of Congas." *Downbeat* (April 21, 1977): 48.

5. Mongo Santamaría, interview, Smithsonian Institution Jazz Oral History Program, 1996.

6. Norbert Goldberg, "An Interview with Mongo Santamaría," *Percussive Notes* (July 1984): 56.

7. The conguero does not read music, so he usually gets a pianist to help him write out the songs.

8. Luis Tamargo, *Mongo's Story*, p. 46. Liner notes to *Skin on Skin: The Mongo Santamaría Anthology 1958–1995* (Rhino Records, 1999).

9. Ibid., pp. 25–26.

10. David Carp, "Barry Rogers: Salsero, Searcher, World Musician," *www.descarga.com*, Profile: Barry Rogers, July 12, 1999.

11. Adrian Pertout, "Herbie Hancock: Watermelon Man," *Mixdown Monthly*, no. 36 (April 9, 1997).

12. Mongo Santamaría, interview, Smithsonian Institution Jazz Oral History Program, 1996.

13. Marco Canihuante, "Marty Sheller Presents," *Ache*, vol. 2, no. 4 (1997): pp. 5–7.

14. Luis Tamargo, "Refuting a Baseless Mythology," *Latin Beat*, vol. 1, no. 10 (November 1991): p. 13.

15. Arnold J. Smith, "Mongo Santamaría: Cuban King of Congas," *Downbeat* (April 21, 1977): 20.

16. Cristobal Díaz Ayala, *Música Cubana del Areyto a la Nueva Trova* (San Juan: Editorial Cubanacan, 1981), p. 339. Migene Gonzalez-Wippler, "Do You Remember the Cheetah?," *Latin N.Y.* (April 1984): 28–30.

17. Smith, "Mongo Santamaría: Cuban King of Congas," pp. 19–20.

18. Willie Colón, "Subject: Salsa One More Time!!! was Re: Héctor Lavoe," rec.music.afro-latin (newsgroup), June 18, 1998.

19. Ibid.

20. Ibid.

21. Tamargo, "Refuting a Baseless Mythology," p. 13.

CHAPTER 8

1. Danilo Lozano, "The Charanga Tradition in Cuba: History, Style, and Ideology." Unpublished dissertation, UCLA, 1990, pp. 180–81.

2. Robin D. Moore, *Nationalizing Blackness: Afrocubanismo and Artistic Revolution in Havana, 1920–1940* (Pittsburgh: University of Pittsburgh Press, 1997), p. 99.

3. Ibid., p. 10.

4. Ibid., p. 39.

5. Ibid., p. 156, bottom picture.

6. Olavo Alén Rodríguez, "The Afro-French Settlement and the Legacy of Its Music to the Cuban People," in Gerald H. Behague, ed., *Music and Black Ethnicity: The Caribbean and South America* (Miami: University of Miami North-South Center, 1994), p. 111.

7. " 'Chico, lleva a Arcaño, que es bueno.' Y los blancos nos contrataban," Erena Hernández, *La Música en Persona* (Havana: Editorial Letras Cubanas, 1986), p. 48.

8. Lozano, "The Charanga Tradition in Cuba," p. 68.

9. Ibid.

10. Gustavo Pérez Firmat, *Life on the Hyphen: The Cuban-American Way* (Austin: University of Texas Press, 1994), p. 100.

11. Ibid., p. 99.

12. Hernández, *La Música en Persona*, p. 51.

13. "Después el bajista no quiso tocar más y también se fue. El pianista se enfermó de trombosis. . . . Ya no tenia personal califado, porque aquí los charangueros son muy pocos. Si uno va hacer una grabación tiene que usar dos violones de Barbarito Diez, otros dos del ICRT . . . y asi." Hernández, *La Música en Persona*, p. 51.

14. See Danilo Lozano, "The Charanga Tradition in Cuba," for an in-depth discussion of the development of the entertainment, broadcasting and recording industries in Cuba in the 1950s and its effects on Cuban music.

15. Leonardo Acosta, cited in Lozano, "The Charanga Tradition in Cuba," p. 71.

16. Yvonne Daniel, *Rumba: Dance and Social Change in Contemporary Cuba* (Bloomington: Indiana University Press, 1995), p. 168, n4.

17. Luis Tamargo, "Mongo Santamaría: Refuting a Baseless Mythology," *Latin Beat*, vol. 1, no. 19 (November 1991).

18. John Storm Roberts, *The Latin Tinge: The Impact of Latin American Music on the United States* (New York: Oxford University Press, 1979), p. 163.

19. Pérez Firmat *Life on the Hyphen*, p. 114.

20. Ibid., p. 99.

21. Ibid., p. 115.

22. Hernández, *La Música en Persona*, p. 38.

23. Miguel Gonzalez-Pando, *The Cuban Americans* (Westport, Conn.: Greenwood Press, 1998), pp. 104–5.

24. Legarreta made these remarks about Fania and the Fania All-Stars when he was interviewed by David M. Carp in 1994. Within a few years after the interview, the Fania All-Stars broke up, Fania Records stopped putting out new releases and its president, Gerry Masucci, died.

CHAPTER 9

1. Miguel Gonzalez-Pando, *The Cuban Americans* (Westport, Conn., Greenwood Press, 1998), pp. 44–46.

2. Silvana Paternostro, interview of Juan Formell, *Bomb* (Winter 2000): 120ff.

3. Arturo Sandoval, telephone interview, August 1999.

4. Peter Manuel, "Musical Pluralism in Revolutionary Cuba," in Manuel, ed., *Essays on Cuban Music: North American and Cuban Perspectives* (Lanham, Md.: University Press of America, 1991), pp. 306–8.

5. Gonzalez-Pando, *The Cuban Americans*, pp. 63–65.

6. Sigfredo Ariel and François Tourtrol, edited by Nigel Williamson. Liner notes to *Eslrellas de Areito: Los Heroes*, Booklet, p. 23 (World Circuit/Nonesuch, 1998).

CHAPTER 10

1. In Cuba, a singer-dancer like Alfonso is called a *vedette*, a word of French origin.

2. "Mi blanca nube. Vuelve a su lecho. La casita azul es el más tierno recuerdo. Nació mi canción entre tristezas y anhelos. Abuela María descansa en el cielo." Juan-Carlos Formell, liner notes to *Songs from a Little Blue House*. Translated by Dita Sullivan (Wicklow Records, 1999).

3. Isabel Leymarie. *La Salsa et le Latin Jazz* (Paris: Presses Universitaires de France, 1993), p. 57.

4. Olavo Alén Rodríguez, *From Afro Cuban Music to Salsa*. Book plus CD (Berlin: Piranha Records), p. 115.

5. "El feeling es una palabra, que no tiene explicación, el feeling es una cosa, que sale del corazón." Cristóbal Díaz Ayala, *Cuando Salí de la Habana 1898–1997: Cien Años de Música Cubana por el Mundo* (San Juan: Fundación Musicalia, 1999), p. 106.

6. Ibid., p. 105.

7. Portuondo does not sing *feeling* with the band, although her reputation as a star in this style is well-known in Cuba.

8. Juan-Carlos Formell, *Songs from a Little Blue House*. Translated by Dita Sullivan (Wicklow Records, 1999).

CHAPTER 11

1. Alfredo "Chocolate" Armenteros, interview, New York City, August 3, 1998. The recorded Armenteros interviews were transcribed into Spanish text and translated into English by Ricardo Luiggi, a professional translator who is knowledgeable about Afro-Cuban/salsa music. Much of the biographical material comes from this and other interviews.

2. James Robbins, "The Cuban *Son* as Form, Genre, and Symbol," *Latin American Music Review* 11 (1990): 182–200.

3. Andy González, interview, Bronx New York, July 29, 1997.

4. Alfredo "Chocolate" Armenteros, interview, New York City, August 3, 1998.

5. Some of these Arsenio Rodríguez recordings have been reissued on the Tumbao Cuban Classics CDs *Dundunbanza* (TCD-043) and *Montuneado* (TCD-0310).

6. *Dundunbanza* (TCD-043).

7. John Storm Roberts, *The Latin Tinge* (Tivoli, N.Y.: Original Music, 1979), p. 114.

8. Andy González, interview, Bronx, New York, July 29, 1997.

9. Beny Moré, *Y Hoy Como Ayer*, BMG/Tropical Series 3203, re-issued 1992.

10. Colin Larkin, ed., *The Guinness Encyclopedia of Popular Music* (New York: Stockton Press, 1995).

11. Donald Clarke, ed., *The Penguin Encyclopedia of Popular Music*, 2nd ed. (London: Viking Press, 1998).

12. Alfredo "Chocolate" Armenteros, interview, New York City, July 20, 1999.

13. Larkin, ed., *The Guinness Encyclopedia of Popular Music*.

14. Peter Manuel, *Caribbean Currents: Caribbean Music from Rumba to Reggae* (Philadelphia: Temple University Press, 1995), p. 74.

15. Roberts, *The Latin Tinge*, pp. 127–31.

16. Ibid., p. 161.

17. Ibid.

18. Manuel, *Caribbean Currents*, p. 74.

19. Roberts, *The Latin Tinge*, p. 164.

20. Vernon W. Boggs, *Salsiology: Afro-Cuban Music and the Evolution of Salsa in New York City* (New York: Excelsior Music, 1992), pp. 203–27.

21. Roberts, *The Latin Tinge*, p. 166.

22. Clarke, *The Penguin Encyclopedia of Popular Music*.

23. Alfredo "Chocolate" Armenteros, interview, New York City, July 20, 1999.

24. Ibid.

Glossary

Bacqueteo. A two-measure pattern consisting of a steady stream of eighth notes played alternatively on various parts of the two timbales drums.

Batá. The principal drums of Santería. Its rhythms are based on a drum language that reproduces the tonal changes and speech patterns of the Yoruba language.

Batalero. Batá player.

Bolero. Slow ballad in salsa.

Bomba. Afro-Puerto Rican genre; name for the drums performing bomba dances. It was adapted by Cortijo in the mid-1950s into a popular dance style and has been taken up by a few salsa musicians.

Bombo. Bass drum played in comparsa; also, the second stroke of the clave.

Bongosero. Bongo player.

Botija. An instrument fashioned from a large ceramic jug into which the performer used his air stream to create the sound. It is tuned by filling it with varying amounts of water. The botija played the bass part in the early *son* groups; it was eventually replaced by the string bass.

Bugalú. Dance style based on the fusion of Afro-Cuban rhythms with the boogaloo, a rhythm popularized by black Americans in the 1960s. The lyrics were sung in English.

Cáscara (literally "rind, shell"). Two-measure pattern played with two sticks ("palitos") on the side of the conga or on a woodblock in rumba, or on the sides of the timbales drums in a salsa group. Other names are gua gua, catá and paila.

Cha cha cha. An off-shoot of the mambo that uses a less-syncopated rhythm. The cha cha cha often features unison singing by the members of the band and has a "sweet" rather than "hot" feeling. The name cha cha cha came from the sound produced by the dancers' sliding feet. Enrique Jorrín wrote the first cha cha cha in 1951.

Charanga. An ensemble with roots in the early part of the twentieth century consisting of flute, piano, bass, violins, güiro and timbales.

Clave. The fundamental rhythmic unit of Cuban music. The clave is a two-measure pattern consisting of three strokes in the first measure and two strokes in the next. The clave pattern is most typically performed on the sticks known as claves. Once established, the two-measure pattern is repeated throughout the performance.

Comparsa. Cuban carnival music performed by a large battery of percussion and brass instruments.

Conguero. Conga player.

Conjunto. A term most often associated with the type of ensemble led by tres player Arsenio Rodríguez in the 1940s. The conjunto evolved from the *son* ensemble of the 1920s and 1930s. The addition of the piano, the conga drum and the creation of a brass ensemble were the main changes.

Coro (literally "chorus"). Passage sung by a chorus of backup singers; section featuring the interplay between a lead singer and the *coro*. The *coro* section is also called the *montuno*.

Danzón. Dance rhythm dating back to the last half of the nineteenth century that evolved from the French contradanse of the eighteenth century.

Descarga. Jam session format developed by Cachao (Israel Cachao López) and other Cuban musicians in the late 1950s.

Guaguancó. A form of rumba in a mid to fast tempo. The guaguancó is a couple dance that pantomimes the man's efforts to seduce a woman and her repulsion of the man. The text of the guaguancó deals with a commentary on everyday life.

Guajeo. A repeated rhythmic vamp typically played by the tres or the piano.

Guía. Verse section. Also called *largo*.

Güiro. A percussion instrument, traditionally a hollowed-out gourd, that is played with a scraper.

Inspiración. Any improvisation, especially a textual improvisation.

Largo. See **Guía**.

Lucumí. Cuban name for people of Yoruba descent.

Mambo (Congolese word for "chant"). A dance style developed in the 1940s. Although the mambos of Arcaño, Arsenio Rodríguez and Pérez Prado were different from each other, they shared one trait: the extensive use of guajeos, which served as a backdrop for instrumental solos and polyphonic exchanges between groups of instruments. Also, the name of the instrumental section that follows the montuno in a salsa arrangement.

Maracas. Handheld rattles or shakers made from gourds filled with beans.

Marimbula.   An instrument, with African roots, that is built along the architectural designs of the mbira or thumb piano. Metal strips of various lengths are fastened to a large resonating wooden box. The performer sits on the box and plays notes by plucking the metal bars.

Martillo (literally "hammer").   The basic rhythm of the bongos.

Merengue.   The fast national dance of the Dominican Republic. Merengue arrangements use simple triadic harmonies rather than the jazz harmonies of salsa.

Moña.   A short repetitive horn line, either written or improvised.

Montuno (literally "rustic").   A short repeating four-or eight-measure phrase, based on a simple chord progression, that contains the call-and-response portion of a piece.

Mozambique.   Name given by Cuban bandleader Pello el Afrokán to his conga rhythm music of the early 1960s.

Orisha.   Deity in the Santería religion.

Orquesta típica ("typical orchestra").   Cornet-led ensemble popular in the late nineteenth and early twentieth centuries. The orquesta típica consisted of various woodwinds and brass instruments, a few strings, güiro and a pair of Creole kettle drums.

Paila.   Timbales; see **Cáscara.**

Palo.   Congolese-derived religion practiced in Cuba.

Plena.   Afro-Puerto Rican song form developed in the 1920s having a verse-refrain structure. The plena is often performed in an ensemble featuring the accordion; texts for the plena are topical in nature.

Quinto.   Smallest conga drum.

Rumba.   Afro-Cuban party music that incorporates percussion, dancing and commentary on everyday life. It is performed by an ensemble of three conga drums, palitos (small sticks) and claves with a lead singer and *coro*. The three forms of rumba performed today are the guaguancó, rumba columbia and yambú.

Rumba columbia.   Rumba dance in a very fast 6/8. The rumba columbia is danced by a solo male dancer.

Rumbero.   Musician who performs rumba.

Rumbón.   Street performance of rumba.

Santería.   Yoruba-derived religion practiced primarily in Cuba, Puerto Rico and parts of the United States such as Miami and New York where there are large Cuban American communities.

Segundo.   Middle conga drum. Also called conga and tres golpes.

Septeto.   Same as the sexteto ensemble (see below) with a trumpet added. Septeto style refers to the Cuban trumpet style that developed in the septetos.

Sexteto.   *Son* ensemble developed around 1920 that consisted of tres, guitar, string bass, bongós, maracas and claves. All the musicians sang except the bongosero.

Son.   Ensemble based on a combination of guitars and percussion instruments that developed at the beginning of the twentieth century in Oriente Province, the mountainous easternmost part of Cuba. *Son* compositions begin with a short section called *largo*, in which the lyrics are prearranged; the *largo* is followed by the improvised *montuno*.

Son conjunto. See **Conjunto.**

Soneo. Improvised text of the lead singer (sonero) in salsa and the *son* groups.

Sonero. Lead singer in salsa and the *son* groups.

Songo. Cuban dance rhythm developed in the late 1960s that features a trap set performing timbales figures. Bongos are absent from the rhythm section. The conga player plays a busy-sounding variant of the guaguancó sequence of open tones rather than the tumbao.

Son pregón. A music form derived from the *son* that is based on the calls of the street vendors in Havana.

Tambolero. *Batá* player.

Timbalero. Timbales player.

Típica (literally "typical"). Adjective used to describe music based on older sources, especially Cuban popular music of the 1940s.

Tres. A guitar-like instrument of Cuban origin with three groups of doubled or tripled strings. It is played with a plectrum. Some tres players prefer to use guitars that have been converted into tres instruments by changing the chording and tuning.

Tumbadora. Largest of the three conga drums.

Tumba. Conga drum.

Tumbao. A repeated pattern played by the bass and the congas.

Vacunao. Name given to a dance movement in some forms of rumba in which the man's seduction of his female partner is pantomimed.

Yambú. A form of rumba performed using wooden packing crates. It is a slow couple dance in 4/4 featuring movements in imitation of the gait of old people.

Selected Bibliography

Barnet, Miguel. *Biography of a Runaway Slave*. Translated by W. Nick Hill. Willimantic, Conn.: Curbstone Press, 1994.

Boggs, Vernon W. *Salsiology: Afro-Cuban Music and the Evolution of Salsa in New York City*. New York: Excelsior Music, 1992.

Chediak, Nat. *Diccionario de Jazz Latino*. Madrid: Edición de Fernando Trueba, Fundación Autor, 1998.

Clarke, Donald, ed. *The Penguin Encyclopedia of Popular Music*, 2nd Edition. London: Viking Press, 1998.

Daniel, Yvonne. *Rumba: Dance and Social Change in Contemporary Cuba*. Bloomington and Indianapolis: University of Indiana Press, 1995.

Fernández, Olga. *Strings and Hide*. Havana: Editorial José Martí, 1995.

Gerard, Charley with Marty Sheller. *Salsa: The Rhythm of Latin Music*. Tempe, Ariz.: White Cliffs Media, 1998.

Gonzalez-Pando, Miguel. *The Cuban Americans*. Westport, Conn.: Greenwood Press, 1998.

Hernández, Erena. *La Música en Persona*. Havana: Editorial Letras Cubanas, 1986.

Kutzinski, Vera M. *Sugar's Secrets: Race and the Erotics of Cuban Nationalism*. Charlottesville and London: University Press of Virginia, 1993.

Lockwood, Lee. *Castro's Cuba, Cuba's Fidel: An American Journalist's Inside Look at Today's Cuba*. New York: Vintage Books, 1969.

Loza, Steven. *Tito Puente and the Making of Latin Music*. Urbana and Chicago: University of Illinois Press, 1999.

Lozano, Danilo. "The Charanga Tradition in Cuba: History, Style, and Ideology." Unpublished dissertation, UCLA, 1990.

Manuel, Peter. *Caribbean Currents: Caribbean Music from Rumba to Reggae.* Philadelphia: Temple University Press, 1995.

Manuel, Peter, ed. *Essays on Cuban Music: North American and Cuban Perspectives.* Lanham, Md.: University Press of America, 1991.

Martré, Gonzalo. *Rumberos de Ayer: Musicos Cubanos en Mexico 1930 a 1950.* Veracruz, Mexico: Instituto Veracruzano de Cultura, 1997.

Mason, John. *Orin Orisa: Songs for Selected Heads.* New York: Yoruba Center, 1992.

Moore, Robin D. *Nationalizing Blackness: Afrocubanismo and Artistic Revolution in Havana, 1920–1940.* Pittsburgh: University of Pittsburgh Press, 1997.

Moreno Vega, Marta. "The Yoruba Orisha Tradition Comes to New York City," *African American Review*, vol. 29, no. 2 (Summer 1995).

Murphy, Joseph M. *Santeria: African Spirits in America.* Boston: Beacon Press, 1988.

Ortiz, Fernando. *La Africanía de la Música folklórica de Cuba.* Havana: Publicaciones Del Minestero de Educacion, 1950. Reprinted Madrid: Editorial Música Mundana Maqueda, SL, 1998.

Pérez Firmat, Gustavo. *Life on the Hyphen: The Cuban-American Way.* Austin: University of Texas Press, 1994.

Robbins, James. "The Cuban *Son* as Form, Genre, and Symbol." *Latin American Music Review* 11 (1990).

Roberts, John Storm. *The Latin Tinge: The Impact of Latin American Music on the United States.* New York: Oxford University Press, 1979.

Ruf, Elizabeth. "Issues of Gender, Color, and Nationalism in Cuba's Tropicana Nightclub Performance." *The Drama Review* 41, no. 1 (Spring 1997).

Thomas, Hugh. *Cuba: Or the Pursuit of Freedom.* New York: Da Capo Press, 1998.

Index

About the Author and Contributors

CHARLEY GERARD is the author of *Jazz in Black and White: Race, Culture and Identity in the Jazz Community* (Praeger, 1998). With Grammy Award-winning arranger Marty Sheller he wrote *Salsa! The Rhythm of Latin Music* (1989, revised 1998). This book was among the first to contain an extensive study of *clave*, the rhythm pattern that gives Cuban popular music and its offshoot, salsa, their distinctive flavor. Besides being an author, Gerard is a saxophonist and composer. His orchestral works are published by Hartelu Music.

GEORGE RIVERA is a freelance writer covering all aspects of the music industry. He has been involved in researching and documenting Latin music for well over 25 years. His work has been published in the United States and throughout Europe. He is currently the music editor at *Salsaweb.com*, an internet-based Latin music magazine.

RICHARD DAVIES is a trombonist and composer who has performed in a myriad of musical contexts. On the Afro-Caribbean and Latin jazz scenes, he has performed with many artists and groups and recorded on over one hundred albums. He was recently appointed Assistant Professor of Music at Plattsburgh State University of New York and is working on a book on the Afro-Cuban and salsa brass tradition.